Improvement by Design

Improvement by Design

The Promise of Better Schools

DAVID K. COHEN, DONALD J. PEURACH,
JOSHUA L. GLAZER, KAREN E. GATES,
AND SIMONA GOLDIN

The University of Chicago Press   Chicago and London

KH

DAVID K. COHEN is the John Dewey Collegiate Professor of Education and professor of education policy at the University of Michigan as well as visiting professor of education at Harvard University. He is the author of several books, most recently *Teaching and Its Predicaments*. **DONALD J. PEURACH** is assistant professor of educational studies in the School of Education at the University of Michigan. He is the author of *Seeing Complexity in Public Education*. **JOSHUA L. GLAZER** is visiting associate professor of education administration at the Graduate School of Education and Human Development at George Washington University. **KAREN E. GATES** was a senior area specialist in the study of instructional improvement at the University of Michigan. **SIMONA GOLDIN** is a research specialist at Teaching Works and a lecturer in the School of Education, both at the University of Michigan.

The University of Chicago Press, Chicago 60637
The University of Chicago Press, Ltd., London
© 2014 by The University of Chicago
All rights reserved. Published 2014.
Printed in the United States of America

23 22 21 20 19 18 17 16 15 14   1 2 3 4 5

ISBN-13: 978-0-226-08924-9 (cloth)
ISBN-13: 978-0-226-08938-6 (paper)
ISBN-13: 978-0-226-08941-6 (e-book)
DOI: 10.7208/chicago/9780226089416.001.0001 (e-book)

Library of Congress Cataloging-in-Publication Data

    Improvement by design : the promise of better schools / David K.
Cohen, Donald J. Peurach, Joshua L. Glazer, Karen E. Gates, and
Simona Golden.
        pages cm
    Includes bibliographical references and index.
    ISBN 978-0-226-08924-9 (cloth : alk. paper) —
    ISBN 978-0-226-08938-6 (pbk. : alk. paper) —
    ISBN 978-0-226-08941-6 (e-book)   1. Educational change—United
States. 2. School management and organization—United States.
I. Cohen, David K., 1934– II. Peurach, Donald J., 1962– III. Glazer,
Joshua L. IV. Gates, Karen E. V. Goldin, Simona.
    LA210.1577 2014
    370.973—dc23   2013014687

⊖ This paper meets the requirements of ANSI/NISO Z39.48-1992
(Permanence of Paper).

9/8/15

To the staff, teachers, and school leaders of the Accelerated Schools Project, America's Choice, and Success for All, from whom we learned so much about improving America's public schools.

Contents

Preface

The primary purpose of this book is to use the analysis of recent school improvement programs to illuminate key issues likely to bear on the enactment of the Common Core State Standards Initiative (CCSSI). We write for policy makers, practicing educators and reformers, and educational researchers whose attention is sure to be occupied by the Common Core for the foreseeable future.

Arguably the most ambitious education reform initiative in US history, the Common Core State Standards Initiative—a state-led coalition of interest groups advancing internationally benchmarked standards for student performance—has swept to prominence like no education reform initiative before it. At the time of this writing, the Common Core Standards have been adopted voluntarily by forty-five states, the District of Columbia, four territories, and the Department of Defense's education activity—a level of coherence in national education reform unthinkable just ten years ago. If the initiative succeeds, it has potential to fundamentally change long-established patterns of teaching and learning, especially in schools that serve many disadvantaged students.

Yet the Common Core Standards are no silver bullet. As made clear by the architects of the initiative (the National Governors Association and the Council of Chief State School Officers) in 2008's *Benchmarking for Success*, the primary idea underlying the Common Core is that shared, internationally benchmarked state standards can propel widespread and coordinated reform of public school systems that are well known to be fragmented and incoherent. With common and ambitious standards in hand, states would leverage their collective influence to improve the quality and coherence of textbooks, curricula, and assessments. They would revise policies for recruiting, preparing, and supporting teachers and school leaders in order to improve the schools' human capital. They would hold schools and districts accountable. And they would intervene and support when schools struggle.

All of these would be enormous changes, and they have gotten considerable attention since the Common Core was launched. Yet there is one other change that has not gotten much attention: the success of the Common Core requires that schools and school systems use these new and (in principle) coordinated resources to make deep change in teaching and learning. Indeed, schools' and systems' constructive response will be the sine qua non of success for the Common Core State Standards Initiative. Yet these are the very schools and school systems that are thought to be doing so poorly that they require the fundamental changes that the Common Core proposes.

There are reasons to be hopeful. There are reasons to be cautious.

From one perspective, the Common Core initiative can be viewed as a radical advance in US education reform. From another perspective, the initiative appears to sustain a logic of systemic reform that has been in motion for nearly a quarter century. The initial articulation of this logic lies in a seminal 1991 essay by Marshall Smith and Jennifer O'Day on standards and accountability as the impetus for the coordinated reforms that they argued were needed to support school-wide improvement. The enactment of this logic was initiated in 1994, with the passage of the Goals 2000: Educate America Act and the Improving America's Schools Act. Policy makers soon doubled down on this logic with the passage of the No Child Left Behind Act of 2001.

Yet, as we've seen over the past quarter century, the historically fragmented and incoherent environments of US public education do not immediately snap into alignment with newly created standards, tests, and accountability standards. Indeed, if the past quarter century is any indicator, the next quarter century of educational reform under the Common Core initiative might *not* feature the rapid emergence of coordinated resources but a sort of reform-induced turbulence, as agencies and organizations within and beyond the K–12 governance structure scramble to apprehend, interpret, and respond to the Common Core. These things would not happen chiefly because educators, policy makers, and others would resist the reforms, but because they would be using the knowledge, skills, and dispositions that worked in the old educational and political order as they tried to understand and operate in the fundamentally different environment that the Common Core seeks to create.

A key part of that problem is that responding positively to reforms and the turbulence they bring is not something that many schools and school systems will know how to do—at least that has been the case for the past quarter century. While school turnaround may be the goal, recent experience suggests that it has been elusive, as evidenced by skyrocketing school failure rates under No Child Left Behind.

In the words of Meredith Honig and Thomas Hatch, the capability to "craft coherence" appears to be unequally distributed among schools. That capability includes setting school-wide goals and strategies; using those goals and strategies to decide whether to bridge or buffer external demands; and constructing district-level support for school-level initiatives. Indeed, in schools that serve many disadvantaged students, reform-induced environmental turbulence has long interacted with persistent fragmentation and incoherence to undermine rather than support the development of these capabilities and the coherence they could bring.

That is one of the chief problems that the Common Core initiative will face. While its architects are clear about the imperative for intervention and supports for struggling schools and systems, the specifics of these resources are much less clear, as are how weak schools and systems could successfully understand and use the new resources. Yet it is on precisely such matters that the success of the Common Core will depend: how can schools and systems that have been too weak to improve on their own use new resources to respond constructively to new, demanding policies?

Note that we describe this as a "chief problem" and not a "fatal flaw." For if the past quarter century provides evidence suggesting the probability of struggles under the Common Core, it also provides evidence of potential for success. This book presents precisely such evidence—that is, how weak schools can improve under the press of external standards in troubled-and-reforming environments. We examine three organizations that were developed and that operated amid the systemic reform movement that preceded the Common Core: the Accelerated Schools Project (ASP), America's Choice (AC), and Success for All (SFA). We analyze how these organizations designed, implemented, improved, and sustained school-wide programs that aimed to help high-poverty elementary schools improve in precisely the ways implied by the Common Core.

Though some might say that the three organizations belonged to an earlier era, they have adapted to changes in policy and the political economy of schooling, and, at the time of this writing, all continue to operate in some form. Success for All remains a leading reform initiative. It was one of four recipients of the largest scale-up grants in the 2010 federal Investing in Innovation (i3) program; a partner with Old Dominion University in the only scale-up grant awarded under the 2011 i3 program; and the recipient of a second 2011 i3 development grant. After being purchased by Pearson—one of the largest organizations in education—in 2010, America's Choice serves as the foundation for Pearson's School-wide Improvement Model, which is among a set of school improvement services that Pearson has devised in response to the Common Core. The Accelerated Schools Project reorganized as AS Plus in the mid-2000s with several hundred schools using the design. At last report, the organization is preparing to launch a new national training center in Durham, North Carolina.

One reason that these programs survived is compelling scientific evidence that SFA and AC succeeded. They improved high-poverty elementary schools; they sustained improvements in leadership, instruction, and student achievement; and they did these things at a large scale. Moreover, the evidence has withstood the rigors of peer review and meta-analyses. In what follows, we present the story behind that success: We examine both how AC and SFA devised programs that helped several thousand of America's weakest elementary schools to make coordinated improvement and why ASP struggled to achieve comparable success.

One important point that follows from our analysis is that the strategy used by all three of these organizations continues to be widely supported for effecting large-scale school improvement: a strategy that we call "improvement by design." This strategy serves as the foundation for school improvement networks in which a central organization develops a common design for school-wide improvement and then collaborates with large numbers of schools to implement, improve, and sustain that design over time. This strategy is currently being used by organizations operating beyond the formal K–12 governance structure: for example, charter management organizations, education management organizations, and comprehensive school reform providers. It is also currently being used by agencies operating within the formal K–12 governance structure: for example, state, regional, and local education agencies assisting schools in enacting Multi-Tier Systems of Supports that structure assessment and intervention around school-wide academic and behavioral programs.

We do not offer a set of how-to prescriptions in what follows. Rather, we offer evidence of how improvement by design can be a strategy to support large numbers of weak schools; of the time it takes to bring programs based on this strategy to fruition; and of the learning required to do so—not only by schools but also by the organizations that seek to support them.

This research was conducted within the Study of Instructional Improvement (SII), fielded at the University of Michigan by the Consortium for Policy Research in Education. SII was a longitudinal, mixed methods study of three leading comprehensive school reform programs that were developed and rose to prominence between the late 1980s and mid-2000s: the Accelerated Schools Project, America's Choice, and Success for All.

Our research and this book would not have been possible without considerable support. We thank the funders of SII: Atlantic Philanthropies USA; the William and Flora Hewlett Foundation; the US Department of Education; and the National Science Foundation's Interagency Educational Research Initiative. We also thank our many colleagues on SII, especially Brian Rowan and Deborah Loewenberg Ball, who, with David K. Cohen, were coprincipal investigators. And we thank the teachers, school leaders, staff members, and managers of the three designs for their many years of collaboration and support. Though we learned much through our collaboration with both colleagues and research participants, we are responsible for all errors of fact and analysis in this book.

ONE

Improvement by Design

This is an account of the common puzzles encountered by three organizations as they built functional educational systems whose aims were to improve many schools attended by many poor children. One puzzle concerned the design of their programs and organizations. A second concerned the implementation of their programs. A third puzzle concerned improving their organizations and programs. A fourth puzzle concerned sustaining their organizations and programs.

All three organizations used a strategy of "improvement by design": that is, improving schools through comprehensive, externally developed interventions. The three interventions—America's Choice, the Accelerated Schools Project, and Success for All—were unusual in their focus and scope. Each sought to effect simultaneous, coordinated change in the day-to-day practices of students, teachers, and school leaders through simultaneous, coordinated change in the roles of those who worked in schools, in the structures and culture in which they worked, and in the technologies of schooling.

The interventions were developed in the 1980s and 1990s, with the goal of greatly improving many of America's weakest schools. They sought teaching that would help students do academically demanding work and boost student achievement. Each was developed and revised in light of experience, in order to improve effectiveness and ensure continued viability in political and economic environments that changed rapidly and often unpredictably.

Each was sponsored and operated by a private organization that was devoted chiefly or entirely to improving education for disadvantaged children. To distinguish these interveners from their interventions, we will refer to the interveners as AC (the organization that developed America's Choice), ASP (the organization that developed the Accelerated Schools Project), and SFA (the organization that developed Success for All).[1]

These three interveners operated alternative school systems of a sort, offering schools across the country designs for change, professional education, help with implementation, support for communication, and new professional standards. They operated on an unprecedented scale. At their peak of operations, each intervener reported supporting a state-sized system of elementary schools: 1,600 elementary schools for SFA (more than the state of New Jersey); 1,400 elementary schools for ASP (more than North Carolina); and 600 elementary schools for AC (more than Arkansas).

All three interveners agreed that improved learning meant moving instruction away from basic skills toward higher-level thought, and that low-achieving students' learning should be accelerated. Yet each of the interveners put the aim of dramatically improved achievement for disadvantaged students in its own terms. SFA sought on-grade reading by the end of third grade. ASP sought "to bring *all* students into the educational mainstream by the end of elementary school, and to build on those gains at subsequent levels."[2] AC expected much more demanding work for all students in reading, writing, and mathematics, as expressed in its performance standards.

Another extraordinary ambition was to raise the bar without requiring vast new resources, such as extended school days, longer school years, or additional teachers. Rather, the three interveners intended to reach their goals by taking schools pretty much as they were: with standard schedules and with the same resources as other high-poverty schools.

The three interveners thus aimed to do what had never been done and what many believed could not be done: take schools that often were educationally quite weak and attended by America's poorest children and make them successful. The schools that had America's biggest educational problems would have to solve them.

That is a common dilemma: policy makers and others can define problems and devise solutions, but only the people and organizations that "are" the problem can solve them, perhaps with help from others.[3] After all, organizations such as AC, ASP, and SFA could no more "improve" schools than teachers could "learn" students. The three interveners faced a particularly difficult version of the dilemma, since the schools with which they worked not only had many weaknesses but also subsisted in environments that contributed to the problems.

One of those problems was very mobile students and teachers: after a year or two of work, a large fraction of the people who had begun to learn the interventions' new approaches would have left, replaced by students and teachers who knew nothing of them. Though students entered school eager to learn, many lacked the academic skills and knowledge typical of more advantaged students; the achievement gap began before students entered school, so teachers' work was harder than in schools that enrolled students from privileged families. High-poverty schools also had much more than their fair share of teachers who had been weak students themselves, who had attended some of the least demanding colleges and universities, and whose professional education was weak. Local districts typically permitted more experienced and qualified teachers to select assignments at less difficult schools, and they did not assign more able teachers to needy schools. High-poverty schools also had, on average, weaker academic leadership and poorer morale.[4]

These were formidable problems, but the interveners were determined to help schools solve them. Support for their work was one reason that they could do it. Indeed, the three interventions were born amid optimism about the potential to improve weak schools as well as policy pressure to do so. This combination of optimism and pressure was well represented in a succession of loosely coordinated policy and philanthropic initiatives that provided billions of dollars (and much legitimacy) to support systemic, comprehensive educational reform for over two decades:

- In 1988, the Hawkins-Stafford Amendments to Title I of the federal Elementary and Secondary Education Act (ESEA) established new goals for improving the academic content and achievement of poor students, and it shifted the unit of improvement from individual students to whole schools. It also opened up new potential for schools with large populations of poor students to use Title I funds for school-wide improvement.
- In 1991, the New American Schools Development Corporation (later rebranded New American Schools, or NAS) was launched as a $130 million, private/public collaboration that championed the development, demonstration, and scale-up of a small number of research-based, "break the mold" designs for comprehensive school reform.
- In 1994, the Goals 2000: Educate America Act established the framework for systemic reform by (among other things) providing grants to states to support the development of performance standards and accountability assessments intended to motivate and support deep-reaching, school-wide improvement.

3

- Also in 1994, the reauthorization of ESEA as the Improving American Schools Act (IASA) repeated the systemic reform framework of Goals 2000, increased the number of schools that could use Title I funds to support school-wide improvement, and established "adequate yearly progress" as the standard by which improvement would be measured (though absent a firm schedule for local or state compliance).
- In 1997, the federal Obey-Porter Comprehensive School Reform Demonstration Act (CSRD) provided $150 million per year that could be used in combination with Title I funds to support comprehensive school reform through state competitive grants, with $145 million to go directly to schools.
- In 1998, the federal Reading Excellence Act (REA) amended Title II of IASA to create a second, new, state-level competitive grant program to support improvement of K–3 reading in the nation's lowest-performing elementary schools. REA provided additional funding that could be combined with both Title I and CSRD funding to support school-wide improvement: $260 million in FY1999 and FY2000, $241.1 million of which went to states.
- In 2002, the reauthorization of ESEA as the No Child Left Behind Act (NCLB) established aggressive national goals for improving the academic achievement of all subgroups of students, increased the resources and incentives provided to states to establish standards and accountability systems, and further increased the number of schools that could use Title I funds to pursue school-wide improvement. Moreover, it incorporated both CSRD and REA into ESEA (the former as the Comprehensive School Reform program and the latter as Reading First) and, in doing so, greatly increased the federal rhetoric supporting "research-based" and "research-validated" school improvement.
- In 2007/8, NCLB was due for reauthorization, like all versions of ESEA before it. However, with problems in its implementation, and with increasing political conflict about the act, reauthorization was politically impossible at that time (and remains so at the time of this writing). The effect was to sustain both accountability pressure and Title I funding that, for over two decades, had motivated and supported comprehensive, school-wide reform.

These policy changes were paralleled by states' adoption of systemic reforms, by judicial action that spurred whole-school reform (specifically, in New Jersey's Abbott districts), and by the growth of private professional groups that urged reform. This all was buoyed by a roaring dot-com economy that—given the growing national focus on school reform—led philanthropists to support school improvement.

This political and fiscal support was instrumental in the emergence not only of SFA, AC, and ASP but also of a larger population of comprehensive school reform providers pursuing their own approaches to "improvement by design." Indeed, nearly seven hundred organizations submitted proposals to participate in the New American Schools initiative, from which eleven were initially selected. Some sought to pursue more "technical-first" solutions: for example, by intervening directly on the day-to-day work of students, teachers, and school leaders, with the resulting success serving as a foundation for building a new culture of high expectations, professional responsibility, and mutual trust. Others sought to pursue more "social-first" solutions: for example, by intervening directly on the social make-up of the school and its relationships with parents and community constituents, with a new culture of trust, expectations, and responsibility providing a foundation for improving the day-to-day work of students, teachers, and school leaders.

But there was much less educational support for these reformers than there was political and fiscal support: that is, support for solving the deep, interdependent problems that had undermined learning, teaching, and leadership in many schools. Quite the contrary, many of these problems had deep roots in the schools themselves as well as their environments. The education of teachers was generally weak, leaving most with a very modest grasp of how to teach academic subjects well. The education of school leaders also was weak; few had a deep grasp of how to lead quality instruction or improve schools.[5] Most districts and states had little capability for school improvement. There were very large inequalities in funding for schools within and among states and among schools within districts, so the schools with the greatest need to improve typically began with the weakest resources to do so.

The central educational problem, however, was that US schools and school systems lacked the wherewithal to make large-scale instructional improvement. Public education never developed the educational infrastructure that is common in school systems in many developed nations: common curricula or curriculum frameworks, common examinations that are tied to the curricula, common educational practices that are grounded in the curriculum, teacher education that focuses on helping teachers learn how to teach the curricula that students will study, and a teaching force whose members had succeeded with those curricula and exams as students, among other things.

Teachers and school leaders who work with such infrastructure have instruments that they can use to set academic tasks that are tied to curriculum and assessment. They have a framework that can help them to define valid evidence of students' work. They can develop a common vocabulary with which to identify, investigate, discuss, and solve problems of teaching and learning. Hence, they have the elements of common professional knowledge and skill. Most important for our purposes here, school systems with such infrastructure have instruments with which they can exert a consistent influence on instruction, at scale. Some even have agencies with the educational capability to lead and support change.

The existence of such infrastructure does not assure excellent education; that depends on how well the infrastructure is designed and how well educators use it. But its absence posed enormous problems for those who would improve education in the United States. If a school wanted to promote academically demanding work, it would have to devise an infrastructure of its own or adapt one that already existed, including curriculum, student assessments, and professional education to help teachers learn to do the work. Some schools had done that, especially in privileged communities. But given the enormity of the task, most settled for less ambitious and more pedestrian work, especially in poor communities.

If the interveners wanted to help schools or school systems to enact significantly better instruction, they had to devise some version of an infrastructure. They then had to find ways to help schools that had no experience with coherent and ambitious instruction to make good use of that infrastructure. And, finally, they had to find ways to help schools to sustain their effort through changes in staff, local and state and federal policy, and other circumstances. It is no exaggeration to say that these efforts to improve schools had to take on fundamental weaknesses of the US education system.[6]

The interveners took them on. They proposed to help schools that had the nation's deepest educational problems learn how to solve them, and to do so in an environment that offered much money and political pressure but little educational help. Unlike earlier efforts to improve schools, each intervener built large elements of an educational infrastructure, so that schools could have coherent and effective instructional programs. They also built elements of infrastructure to support schools' work, including professional education, communication networks, common professional language and culture, and organizations to support these things. They had to capitalize on political support while coping with many educational barriers in the same environment. It was an extraordinary assignment.

Distinct Designs for Improvement

Each of the interveners did these things differently. One reason our account is so compelling is that the interveners faced common puzzles despite pursuing three distinct approaches to design-based school improvement. The designers of Success for All believed that teachers should first adhere to tightly specified plans and then adapt them as they grew more expert. By contrast, the designers of America's Choice made room for teachers' discretion from the outset while also seeking to increase their knowledge and skills so they could use discretion effectively. The designers of the Accelerated Schools Project believed that once schools had defined their goals in accord with the program's educational philosophy and reorganized, they could exploit existing resources in themselves and the environment.

Success for All

Success for All was founded and developed in 1987/88 by a research group at Johns Hopkins University led by the husband-and-wife team of Robert Slavin and Nancy Madden, both psychologists. The project team and the program were originally headquartered in that university's Center for the Social Organization of Schools. In 1994, the project team moved to the Center for the Study of Students Placed at Risk, also at Johns Hopkins. In 1997/98, the project team left Johns Hopkins to establish the independent, nonprofit Success for All Foundation. True to the professional identify and expertise of its founders, one key aim was to anchor Success for All in practices identified in prior research as both effective and replicable in improving student performance; a second key aim was to constantly evaluate the replicable effectiveness of Success for All and its multiple interacting components.

Drawing on more than a decade of earlier efforts both to synthesize available research and to field targeted programs, the designers of Success for All focused on the creation of a K–6 reading curriculum that matched a detailed design for cooperative learning among students with detailed guidance for direct instruction by teachers. Its designers specified the methods, moves, and steps for effective teaching, so that students would learn more when teachers followed the program's directions. Their early work convinced the designers that a very detailed instructional plan for K–6 reading could initially overcome teachers' weak expertise, create immediate change, and improve students' learning. They believed that those changes would lift teachers' motivation and commitment to the design, building a foundation for teachers to develop much more expert practice in which they exercised more professional discretion, to support even better student achievement. The directions for K–6 reading were detailed, and they were designed to help teachers themselves to learn while they were teaching. That learning would, in a year or two, enable teachers to reduce their dependence on the directions and be more effective on their own. The extensively elaborated directions were a beginning, and the detail was a way to represent effective practice so that any teacher in a high-poverty school could enact it immediately with any student.

Success for All also sought to build schools' organizational capability to improve instruction. A common curriculum would help coordinate instruction within schools by providing materials with which teachers could interact fruitfully over their students' work. It would offer a common vocabulary and syntax for teaching and learning. Professional education offered by each school's instructional leaders (especially the reading facilitators) would also help to create instructional consistency within schools. A chief aim of Success for All was a professional community in which instructional coherence, collective effort, and collective capability would greatly improve students' learning. One can think of the directions for K–6 reading as a way to transfer usable professional knowledge from researchers and capable practitioners to less capable practitioners; the materials were directions for conduct, content for professional education, and glue for coherent instruction.

Accelerated Schools Project

The Accelerated Schools Project was established in 1986 by a team of Stanford University researchers led by economist Henry Levin. In 2000, the project team moved to the University of Connecticut's Neag School of Education.

Like Success for All, the program was anchored in deep concern with improving the educational opportunities for students at risk of academic failure, especially given research that some remedial programs did more to slow the growth of at-risk students than to accelerate it. However, in contrast to Success for All, the designers of the Accelerated Schools Project believed that an externally devised technical infrastructure was not required. They argued that most of the technical resources for better instruction already existed in schools and their environments, and that a crucial failing of most efforts had been the imposition of external solutions. In their view such things often were implemented mechanically and superficially, which blocked deep and lasting change. Hence they saw the key issue as finding a way to help teachers to create a cultural infrastructure, including professional norms and organization, that would enable them to devise their own technical infrastructure with which to deeply change teaching and learning. Only creation from within, not detailed directives from beyond, would enable real change.

The Accelerated Schools Project therefore did not create its own detailed infrastructure for instruction. Instead, it focused the work of school staffs on changing professional culture and school organization so that they could devise change that suited their situations. ASP's designers argued that transformed culture would enable school staffs to build on existing strengths, develop new capabilities, and devise versions of improved instruction that they termed "powerful learning." ASP focused most guidance on whole-school change, so as to replace a culture of failure and remediation with a culture of success and enrichment. School staffs were to use broad participation and consensual decision making to diagnose their problems, set new goals, and devise strategies that would enable them to treat all children as gifted and talented. Once those things were done, school staffs could figure out the specific educational programs that expressed their vision. They might invent their own programs, but the designers of the Accelerated Schools Project saw no shortage of good materials and other educational resources in the environment. With new visions and strategies in hand, educators could invent, adapt, and borrow what they needed for their own instructional infrastructures. Because it would be what all the members of the school accepted, it would be used and sustained.

America's Choice

America's Choice was established by the National Center on Education in the Economy (NCEE) in Washington, DC, under the leadership of Marc Tucker and on the heels of its 1990 report entitled *America's Choice: High Skills or Low Wages*. While also concerned with the educational opportunities and outcomes of at-risk students, the ideas that drove the development of America's Choice were more concerned with adapting the US public education system to a rapidly changing global economy. America's Choice built on two earlier efforts by NCEE: the National Alliance for Restructuring Education, a collaboration with states and districts to develop coordinated capabilities for school improvement; and the New Standards Project, a collaboration with the University of Pittsburgh's Learning Research and Development Center to develop a coordinated system of performance standards and assessments for schools.

Drawing on these earlier efforts, the developers of America's Choice focused on building infrastructure for instruction, as Success for All had done. They argued that schools lacked both clear, rigorous academic goals for all students and strong professional education for teachers. The foundation of America's Choice was a very specific set of outcomes—the New Standards Project's academic standards and reference exams—that set content goals for academic work. America's Choice staff then used those standards and exams to adapt a set of graded, subject-specific instructional frameworks, to guide teaching and learning in the core academic subjects. Detailed performance standards were central. So while Success for All offered detailed guidance for instruction in K–6 reading, and the Accelerated Schools Project focused on culture and organization, America's Choice offered detailed, academically ambitious instructional outcomes, animated by examples of student work. Standards-based instruction was the signature of America's Choice.

The designers of America's Choice valued professional discretion and sought to cultivate it, much as in the Accelerated Schools Project. Yet there was much less room for local invention or adaptation in America's Choice, for its instructional goals and frameworks were clear, and the assignment for the school staff was to learn how to realize them in curriculum and instruction. The Accelerated Schools Project, in contrast, saw instruction as each school's creation, within the broad frame of powerful learning, with much more room for local invention and adaptation. Both sets of designers valued professional discretion, but America's Choice sought to frame teachers' discretion primarily in an explicit infrastructure for instruction rather than primarily in ideas about organization and culture, as ASP did.

In contrast to Success for All, America's Choice did not provide detailed routines for teaching. Its leaders believed that such detailed guidance would inhibit teachers' cultivation of the complex professional knowledge and skills that they would need to help students achieve at much higher levels. Expert teaching required an explicit infrastructure, autonomy, and expert judgment in order to adapt it to specific schools, classrooms, and students. America's Choice sought to create a common frame for instruction, and it had fairly explicit guidance for new practices in written materials and professional education. But instead of detailed directions, there would be standards and outcomes, curriculum frameworks, and extended opportunities for teachers to learn how to turn those elements of infrastructure into effective practice. Where Success for All used materials as a key vehicle for changing knowledge and practice, America's Choice sought to use school-based teacher education.

Common Obstacles to Success

If differences between the interventions proved to be quite important, so too were similarities, including several common obstacles to success.

All three of the interveners focused chiefly on individual schools rather than on school systems or states. The idea that schools were the unit of change was widely accepted in the late 1980s and 1990s, the key point being that, since schools were where learning occurred (or didn't), that was where remedial action should focus. The local districts that create, fund, and regulate schools, and that are legally responsible for them, were thought to be too far from instruction to merit intervention and even a nuisance in improving education.[7]

The interveners also agreed that schools were complex organizations with systemic problems and that these systemic problems called for systemic solutions. The interveners thought that teaching and learning in schools should be coherent, which implied extensive coordination within and among grades and across subject areas. This meant that instruction was connected to schools' organization and leadership, and that significant change in the former required change in the latter. They had very different views about how and what to coordinate, but all saw instruction as a complex system. To intervene only on a single part of schooling, like curriculum, would fail to influence many things that could shape students' learning, like teachers' knowledge and skill, or academic goals, or leadership.

All three of the interveners also sought to help schools solve many problems with a single package. They aimed to turn schools into coherent learning communities that produced high student achievement. That ambition, taken with the schools' many weaknesses, meant that school professionals would need extensive help to learn to use the new designs and to *un*learn many familiar practices and beliefs. The interveners would support them in two ways: by redesigning schools so that student learning itself became a pervasive feature of staff work while at the same time offering staff extensive assistance in learning to work within the redesigned schools. The three interveners thus agreed that school professionals could learn their way out of their problems. They also agreed on their important part in implementation, and they expended a great deal of effort either to support implementation in schools that adopted their programs or to find other agencies that would support it. In these ways and others they explicitly and implicitly tied their own success to that of the schools.

All three interveners also took schools as they found them. They could have opened charter schools with new faculty and students, but they worked with schools that had America's weakest teachers in some of its poorest communities. They did so in part because they thought that systemic designs would be powerful and in part because they saw strength in students' enthusiasm for learning. The three interveners argued that, despite the problems sketched above, all students enter school eager and expecting to learn and that all students can learn rich academic content at high levels. What students *did* learn depended on whether the adults in schools were willing to do everything possible to ensure it. An adage within Success for All captured a key shared idea that the interventions were "1% program and 99% belief system."[8]

All three interveners also proposed to solve problems *in* schools, even though many problems arose outside them. They did not initially deal with district central offices, because those offices had not involved themselves deeply in classroom work. That turned out to be a problem, for local central offices did many things that *did* affect classrooms, including hiring and placing teachers and school principals, adopting curricula and tests, and allocating school budgets. Even though schools were where the instructional action was, central offices were the strongest and most salient element in the schools' environment, and they affected what happened in classrooms.

That isn't to say that central offices were the only environmental obstacles to success. If the interveners were to take schools as they were and still improve learning, teaching would have to improve quite dramatically. But the weakness of teaching in high-poverty schools was due to such environmental factors as weak university teacher education, the lack of strong incentives to teach in such schools, high teacher mobility, and central office habits of assigning the weakest teachers to the most needy schools.[9] Since these factors arose outside individual schools, to take schools as they were was to implicitly agree to a game of everlasting catch-up.

These common obstacles were compounded by the interveners' ambition to improve hundreds or thousands of high-poverty elementary schools. The designers were appalled by the weak education that many poor and minority children received, and they wanted to change it. Yet they did not want to create demonstration programs showing that good things could happen in small, protected places. They wanted good things for many children in many ordinary places, and they sought to work on a large scale. Given the problems just sketched, it would have been very demanding to improve a dozen high-poverty schools; it would be much more demanding to improve several hundred or a thousand such schools.

The interveners saw the difficulty of improving instruction at a large scale, which led them to build complex organizations to support their work. Since ASP believed that many agencies in the environment would support school improvement, it matched a lean central office with a de-centralized support system. Most implementation assistance was to come from local and regional agencies, with the goal of institutionalizing the Accelerated Schools educational philosophy in these local and regional agencies. AC and SFA created complex, self-sustaining organizations that were unusual in their internal professional development for staff, their institutional capabilities and size, the money they raised to support the work, and their long-term viability.

One other similarity concerned the relationship between the interveners and their environments. Although each was organized around a quite distinct vision of good education and how to achieve it, all three aimed to support programmatic coherence within and among schools. Yet all three operated in environments in which such clear visions were quite unusual, in large part because clear and sharp educational visions had provoked much political conflict, and that was something that school systems had learned to avoid.[10] Most schools that are informed by such visions exist in the nonpublic sector, away from the conflicts that have troubled public schools since they began. The three interveners offered a promising way to improve schools, but that meant involving agencies that often had their own internal conflicts.

Indeed, what US schools and school systems had in common was often less programmatic than geographic and jurisdictional. Each local educational agency (LEA) is tied to a locality. Its authority arises from its existence as an agency of government, and it draws its identity, as well as its socioeconomic makeup, from its location. In contrast, the interveners sought to build systems of schools that cohered around common aims, common educational programs, common values and norms, and common methods. Since the interveners lacked formal political authority and geographic integrity, they used organization and communication networks to create and sustain program coherence, visibility, legitimacy, and momentum.

At the same time that the interveners experienced serious conflicts with environments, they also found themselves heavily dependent on those same environments. They had to support their work with money from the environment (including Title I of the ESEA) and from private foundations, and they required at least tacit support from state and lo-cal school systems. The interveners had to balance their wish for vision-driven schooling with many American educators' aversion to such things. They had to balance their intention to do what public school systems rarely had done with their need for good relations with those systems. They had to balance their wish for programmatic coherence with their wish to recruit schools from many varied circumstances. They had to decide how much to adapt (or not adapt) the designs to state and local requirements, and they had to adapt their own organization to work in varied environments. Or, to take the same issue from the other side, schools that enlisted with an intervention had to balance established operations and the demands of their membership in state and local school systems with the requirements of the intervention.

It was not easy to manage this set of balancing acts. Consider the ways in which many schools had long dealt with external interventions. Schools had often adopted a variety of innovations, in part because their environments offered a steady diet of quick fixes. As a result, it was common to find many interventions operating at one time in a single school. Consequently, educators in many schools were unfamiliar with a guiding idea shared by all three interventions: that all work in a school should flow from a coherent and well-coordinated program. Thus, many schools that adopted one of the three interventions did not close down existing, often inconsistent improvement efforts, and some continued to launch new initiatives alongside the interventions. It was one thing for school professionals to promise to make the interventions their top priority, but it was very different and much more difficult to close down existing programs. Work with the interventions was important to schools and districts, but it was in constant conflict with other pressures from their environments.

The conflicts between the interventions and their environments cut deep. On the one hand, while school districts were jurisdictions that had political legitimacy and stable funding, they often lacked common visions or programs. On the other hand, while the interveners had clear visions, common goals, common methods of work, and common professional educations, they lacked political legitimacy or stable funding. Because the interveners lacked those things, they had to operate in the interstices of established systems with which their approach conflicted, and they had to gain that system's support. They tried to build new sorts of vision-driven, mission-oriented school systems inside much larger, vision-neutral, bureaucratic, and inhospitable systems.

Educational Innovation in Historical Context

The scope and boldness of the interveners' ambitions, and the conflicts with their environments, are easier to appreciate if we compare them with earlier efforts to improve schools. Most of those efforts were much less comprehensive and ambitious; they had fewer difficulties because they did not seek changes that environments did not support.

For example, earlier innovators tried to boost students' learning by devising new curricula. Scientists and other scholars invested a great deal of time and talent creating new curricula in science, mathematics, and the humanities in the late 1950s and early 1960s, and they raised a great deal of government money to support the work. They believed that better materials alone could boost students' learning, and they aimed especially to improve education for the most academically able students.[11] Many of their designs were adopted by commercial publishers and sold to schools. Other innovators tried to improve teacher education by creating Masters of Arts in Teaching programs or by devising professional development for teachers already at work. Still others sought to change school finance, investing many years and much legal talent to eliminate fiscal inequality among localities within states. Others devised new approaches to professional development, new ideas about school leadership, new forms of school organization, and the like.

These reforms defined improvement in ways that required action on only one of the many aspects of school programs and, with that, limited their environmental dependencies. New curricula required government funds and interest from commercial publishers, but it did not require attention to teacher education, student mobility, or schools' organization and leadership. School finance reform required attorneys willing to sue states, money to fund their work, and, in some cases, activists willing to lobby state legislatures, but it required no attention to curriculum, teacher education, school organization, and all the other influences on how new funds might be used if the litigation succeeded.

While their limited scope made it possible to advance these reforms, the results were quite partial. Researchers found, for instance, that the new curricula that drew in such scientific talent in the 1950s and 1960s had little effect on student performance, because the developers gave little attention to helping teachers learn how to use them well, and even less to figuring out how schools should change to help teachers use them well. Similarly, though more money could help to improve education in poor districts, the finance reforms gave only a little attention to how the new funds would be used. If the same poorly educated teachers and administrators used new funds in the old ways, which mostly they did, teaching and learning would improve little or not at all.

Some of these innovations were widely adopted, in part *because* they were not comprehensive, or not academically ambitious, or both. A catchy new professional development scheme was relatively easy to devise and adopt. New curricula were difficult to create but they were also relatively easy to adopt, and many *were* widely adopted. There was a ready market for textbooks and professional development. Schools were in the habit of using the former, and many states and localities required professional development days and needed providers. In addition, the organization of schooling—federalism, the separation of powers, and local control—fragmented the market for innovation. Jeffersonian distrust of government meant that states developed little capability to govern or manage schools, and most outsourced the core elements of academic work, like curriculum and tests, to private firms. That further fragmented guidance for instruction. The result was diverse, often contrary, and generally weak guidance. Schemes to improve schools were just another voice in the cacophony, and none offered authoritative support for ambitious improvement.[12]

These things might not have been such a problem had there been other means to focus instruction. If the education professions had sponsored strong education for their members and common standards of practice, teachers could have taught, evaluated student work, and solved problems in ways consistent across the nation, without intensive government oversight. That, however, would have required the educational infrastructure that US schools lacked.

Alternatively, school principals, central office staff, and state education leaders could have been educated as experts in the management of teaching and learning, and used their positions to set standards of quality. But nothing like that existed. Professional education for both teachers and leaders was quite weak and far from coherent. There are many professional standards, but few are geared to practice, and there has been very little oversight of practice. School managers typically knew little about instruction, and they delegated most decisions to teachers. That left teachers fairly free to respond to improvement schemes as they preferred, and few chose ambitious schemes. Most teachers were modestly educated. Those who taught elementary school rarely knew a great deal about the subjects they taught, for few had college majors in literature or mathematics, which comprised most of the elementary school curriculum. High school teachers often did have a college major in the subject they taught, but they learned little about how to help students to learn it. Teachers' preferences quickly became an important part of the environment, and innovators responded.[13]

If there had been strong and consistent pressure for ambitious performance, things might have been different. Had Americans been convinced that schools should hold students to high academic standards, and that teachers were obliged to help students perform well, it is likely that many local schools would have responded, since the public paid the taxes that paid professionals' salaries. Yet until very recently few members of the public seem to have supported ambitious academic performance, and fewer pressed for it, outside of affluent districts with educated and ambitious parents. Reformers could press ambitious change and offer extensive assistance, or offer reforms that made fewer demands on practitioners, or invent programs that might work despite the lack of extensive support. Most chose one of the last two alternatives.

In these circumstances teachers soon found that they could take the advice they preferred, ignore the rest, close the classroom door and teach as they wished. That was useful in a culture in which educational issues and fashions changed regularly: better science and math for the best and brightest in the late 1950s, better schools for poor children in the mid-1960s, minimum competency tests for low-achieving students in the early and mid-1970s, and so on. As professional and political priorities changed, few reform efforts lasted. Those who disliked the innovation du jour could put their heads down, fairly sure that it would soon pass, and be none the worse for it. Teachers could adopt modest schemes to improve instruction, for they could use them more or less as they liked, without great effort. This situation offered innovators incentives to offer attractive promises of easy and quick improvement, not designs that required intensive and sustained effort. Innovators responded accordingly.

Partial and undemanding innovations were well adapted to environments in which schools and teachers could respond as they saw fit. That worked for many teachers who welcomed something new but who were unlikely to push very far into academic subjects or students' thinking about them. It also worked in the sense that many were adopted by state and local school systems, despite—or perhaps because—they could be weakly implemented with no negative consequences. Many worked only briefly, either because they were soon forgotten in the rush for the next new thing or because they ran into problems and were abandoned. Few had any appreciable effect on teaching or learning. The innovations that prospered were modest in ambition and operation. Many issued from university projects whose funds from federal or foundation grants were temporary. Innovation designers had few incentives to make enduring commitments to the enterprise or to help schools with implementation.

These approaches to innovation fit with the idea that schools needed little more than a nudge in the right direction in order to change. The leading scientists who wrote the ambitious new curricula of the 1950s and 1960s assumed that their good ideas and intellectual influence could put schools on a new course. Many reformers and educators saw the funds that Title I sent to localities as a key to school improvement for disadvantaged children. Even as the interventions that we report on here were beginning, in the 1980s and 1990s, school reformers argued that school restructuring—changing decision processes, decreasing size, and reorganizing daily schedules—would enable improvement in even the weakest schools. Few argued that detailed designs, long-term work, and substantial professional support were needed for real improvement.

AC, ASP, and SFA were a stark change. They proposed to help schools renew themselves at a depth and on a scale that never had been attempted. The scope, size, and ambition of their networks and interventions made them unique among existing school systems and previous improvement schemes. No school systems had ever attempted such large scale, comprehensive, and deep-reaching improvement, and no nongovernment agencies had ever tried to build systems of common schools in the interstices of the established systems. Not only did the interveners face much greater problems of implementation than their much more partial cousins, they faced them precisely because their ambitious designs were at such odds with the unsystemic habits of most US schools and their unsystemic environments. The attributes that made the three designs so distinctive and promising made them especially difficult to put into practice.

These points are particularly important because all three interveners assumed that weak schools could use their designs and effectively turn themselves around. The interveners had strongly principled perspectives, and the designs were both carefully worked out and continuously evolving. Even so, the work was novel, demanding, and very uncertain. Nobody knew how comprehensive school reform would play out in difficult schools, for few reformers had even imagined such comprehensive interventions, and fewer still had tried to develop or sustain organizations capable of supporting such deep change. The interventions were as much conjectures as answers, and the interveners could only develop the capabilities to successfully develop and field them by learning from the experience of doing just that.

Qualified Success

AC, ASP, and SFA had qualified success along several dimensions that are as central to the current national agenda for educational reform as they were in the late 1990s. In contrast to categorical programs for students, the three interveners successfully devised comprehensive interventions that took the entire school as the unit of treatment. They achieved a scale of operations that rivaled state education agencies, and they evolved in ways that enabled them to sustain operations in some form for two decades and counting. Finally, though not as strong and consistent as the interveners intended, several independent studies found a pattern of positive program effects on student achievement.[14] The three interventions were among a small group of comprehensive school reform providers that experienced degrees of success along these same dimensions, including those pursuing both technical-first and social-first solutions: for example, Direct Instruction, Core Knowledge, First Things First, the Literacy Collaborative, the National Writing Project, the School Development Program, School Renaissance, and the Talent Development High School model.[15] While some readers may disagree, these are remarkable accomplishments, quite without precedent in US educational history.

Yet comprehensive school reform has had a low profile in contemporary policy discourse, despite ample evidence that these designs can succeed. The low profile is traceable to developments that eroded political support for the designs in the first decade of the twenty-first century. The developments included the planned termination of New American Schools, efforts by the George W. Bush administration to concentrate federal funding in its flagship Reading First program, the subsequent mismanagement of Reading First, the slow pace at which comprehensive school reform programs are designed and developed compared to the rapid issue-attention cycle of US education policy, and many comprehensive school reform programs' inability to complete rigorous evaluations.[16]

That is particularly unfortunate because our colleagues in the Study of Instructional Improvement showed that AC, ASP, and SFA succeeded in moving schools toward more productive leadership and instructional practice. Their studies found that all three interventions successfully configured and activated more complex, distributed schools leadership teams that provided significantly more instructional leadership than comparison schools.[17] The studies also reported that SFA and AC also strongly and broadly changed instruction, which they attributed to the interveners' combining detailed guidance for practice with extensive, practice-based professional learning opportunities.[18]

Our analyses extend those studies. We examine coordinated guidance and professional development as two key elements of the broader educational infrastructure needed to make coordinated improvement in deeply rooted and unproductive leadership and instructional practices, and in student achievement. We also provide detailed, longitudinal analysis of the interveners' work as they created, improved, and sustained this broader educational infrastructure in the turbulent environments of public education. These educational practices will be central to the now developing national agenda for large-scale educational reform, because they are key to schools' and school systems' use of the resources that the Common Core promises.

Yet these educational practices have been little studied and are weakly understood. Why? When they develop—which has been only infrequently—they do so at places that have been difficult to imagine, let alone to find and visit. The experiences of AC, ASP, and SFA reveal that the practices that were essential to improving America's weakest schools occurred at the intersection of several forces: one was the schools' weaknesses; another was the fragmented, weak, and often chaotic educational and political environments; still another was the use of private organization to improve government-sponsored and operated-schools. That intersection is where the interveners worked with schools, and where the strengths and weaknesses of their designs and organizations came into play. To succeed as they did, they had to invent, develop, and deploy practices that enabled them to deal constructively with these forces and the imposing problems that they entailed. That intersection is precisely where good work with the Common Core will occur, if it does occur.

Many legislators, businessmen, and educators seem to believe that school improvement is straightforward: Simply fix the curriculum, or accountability, or leadership, or the quality of teachers, or school finance. These things do need to be fixed, but there is no single or simple fix because they interact with each other; each is part of a systemic problem, and there will be little improvement unless many things come together to support solutions. America's Choice and Success for All devised systemic solutions, they made systemic change, and teaching and learning improved. That is the most significant feature of the account that follows, and the greatest challenge that faces the Common Core: Will politicians and educators invent, adapt, and support interventions that can devise systemic solutions to systemic problems, in the places and with the practices that can make a difference?

Our Account

Our study is a comparative analysis of the interveners, their designs, their organizations and their networks. It runs for more than a decade, from the time of their inception to the close of our study in 2008. The year 2008 proved an active one for federal education policy: it was the year in which a reauthorized No Child Left Behind was to have taken effect, had the reauthorization proceeded on schedule; and it was the year of transition from the Bush to the Obama administration, a transition that helps to explain why ESEA/NCLB wasn't reauthorized. It was also an active year for state education policy, as the National Governors Association and the Council of Chief State School Officers released *Benchmarking for Success*, which laid the foundation for the Common Core State Standards Initiative.

Our primary purpose is to provide policy makers, practicing educators, reformers, and educational researchers with a perspective on the central challenge of the Common Core: how to create, manage, and sustain the standards-aligned educational infrastructure that could support improved leadership, instruction, and student achievement in many schools.

The interveners took on tough work in their efforts to support improvement in high-poverty schools, and it was complicated to understand and explain their operations and experience. The three interveners did exceedingly complex work, for it spanned many actors in many schools, school systems and states, the designers' organizations, many private and public agencies in the environment, and it extended over more than two decades. Part of the complexity, as this recitation reveals, was how interdependent the work was.

To gain some purchase on this unusual complexity, we centered our research in a way that was somewhat unique in educational research: we focused on the interveners. Many researchers study the implementation and effects of externally developed programs, but few centered their data collection and analysis on the external interveners over long periods of time. Our aim in this was to deepen understanding of improvement by design as a strategy for large-scale, practice-focused, school improvement. In fact, the few accounts of such work that do exist are largely those of program developers themselves, which lack the independence of an external study team.[19]

Moreover, we maintained this perspective for a very long time, from 1996, when we first began sampling programs for participation in the Study of Instructional Improvement, through 2008. During those twelve years, we analyzed mountains of documents and materials, spent hundreds of days in participant-observation of training sessions and school visits, conducted more than one hundred formal interviews, and had thousands of informal conversations with school and intervention staff members. The appendix offers a complete account of our research methods.

Between 1996 and 2008, we used our iterative data collection and analysis to devise a framework for analysis that increased our ability to see order amid the swirls of the ongoing work.[20] We saw that both the successes and struggles of all three interveners arose through complex interactions in four domains of activity:

- The *schools* that the interveners sought to serve;
- The *designs* that they constructed to support their improvement;
- The *organizations* that they created to develop and field those designs;
- The *environments* in which schools, the designs, and the interveners operated.

Each of these domains and the interactions among them were a source of opportunity and strength. Yet each domain and the interactions among them also were a source of obstacles and weakness. What is more, these domains did not interact in predictable, tractable, and consistent ways across the three interventions. Rather, they pushed against each other in often unpredictable and difficult to discern ways, because they varied with interveners' purposes, strategies, histories, geographic location, and more.

For example, a seemingly transparent improvement to a design proved difficult to implement in schools. This created the need to develop new training capabilities in the intervener's organization, which in turn required new funding from agencies in the environment. An adjustment in the reporting of state assessment scores in two or three states changed the distribution of schools that appeared to be succeeding and struggling, and so required adaptations to software and other program resources, and the adaptation of training and support services. Major changes in federal policy rattled schools, designs, the intervening organizations, and district and state policy contexts simultaneously, with decisions about how best to respond contingent on how others decided to respond.

These things were constant over the entire existence of the interventions and our entire period of observation. As our data collection and analysis developed, we saw that the interveners' work was framed by four core puzzles that seem to be endemic to improvement by design.

- The *design puzzle* centers on efforts to construct plans and blueprints for developing coherence and capabilities among schools, designs, intervening organizations, and environments, with the goal of supporting improvement in practice and achievement.

- The *implementation puzzle* centers on what happens when plans and blueprints are put into motion, including the unanticipated and dysfunctional interactions that arise among schools, designs, intervening organizations, and environments.
- The *improvement puzzle* develops from efforts to understand and address those unanticipated and dysfunctional interactions, in order to improve technical effectiveness.
- The *sustainability puzzle* also develops from efforts to address those unanticipated and dysfunctional interactions, though with the goal of maintaining the interventions' viability in complex, turbulent, and uncertain environments.

We labeled these "puzzles" because they were exactly that, in every sense of the word. Moving our work forward required understanding how many different, interdependent pieces were and weren't working together to create some larger, more coherent wholes. However, there was no picture in the research manual—and no manual—to provide guidance either for the interveners or for ourselves. Instead, the interveners began work with weak knowledge about what they were attempting, and we followed in their wake. While they began their efforts on the heels of extensive research on program implementation, and while researchers worked feverishly and contemporaneously to generate knowledge about what was happening with comprehensive school reform, the great bulk of that research did very little to provide practical guidance for addressing the strategic and operational issues that came with managing a state-sized school improvement network. Further, actually heeding key findings from emerging research often exacerbated their strategic and operational problems. One example was managing the cross-pressures between calls to improve fidelity of implementation (on the one hand) and to adapt the interventions to local districts' preferences (on the other) in order to make them key partners in program implementation.

Our challenge was to devise a way to structure our account of the interveners so as to best portray the uncertainty and complexity of their work. In doing so, our objective was *not* to make exhaustive use of our vast data and analyses. Doing so would have required book-length accounts of each of the three interventions. And, in fact, we *have* produced three such accounts under separate cover (specifically, one book and two dissertations), along with multiple journal articles and conference presentations that support key points made in this book. Rather, our objective was to use our data and analyses judiciously to develop and explain our most central analytic points.

One option would have been to organize our account in the form of an edited volume: that is, as three intervention-specific chapters, matched with an introduction and conclusion that pulled key themes from each of these accounts. This approach has been used in leading accounts that feature the self-reports of individual program developers.[21]

We experimented with this approach, but we found that it did more to emphasize the distinctness of each intervention than it did to make vivid what we viewed as the most important and compelling lesson to be drawn from our analysis: *that the three interveners experienced common puzzles despite formidable differences in their approaches to design-based school improvement.* Moreover, representing that lesson within such a structure would have created the arduous task, for authors and readers, of connecting points of comparison that often appeared twenty or thirty pages apart, stretched across multiple chapters.

So instead we opted to use the four puzzles to structure an analytic narrative account of the experiences of AC, ASP, and SFA that would place the four puzzles in the foreground and clarify their salience to the interveners' experience. Within each chapter, we detail how differences in the purposes, strategies, and experiences of each intervener resulted in intervention-specific manifestations of each puzzle. We summarize the chapters below.

Chapter 2 details the design puzzle that the interveners plunged into amid early enthusiasm and support for comprehensive school reform. Chapter 3 details the implementation puzzle that they faced as their carefully constructed blueprints were put into motion in thousands of newly recruited schools. Chapter 4 details the improvement puzzle that manifested amid the opportunities and pressures of NCLB. Chapter 5 details the sustainability puzzle in which the interveners adapted their enterprises to maintain currency and viability in multiply uncertain environments. Finally, chapter 6 details the primary lessons that we draw from our analysis of the interveners' work.

By using this puzzle-oriented structure, we extend the work of Joseph P. McDonald, Emily J. Klein, and Meg Riordan, who used a similar structure to depict the challenges identified in a single-site case study of a leading, network-based initiative—the Big Picture Company—in going to scale.[22] One of our coauthors used a close cousin of the puzzles framework to structure a stand-alone study of Success for All, by highlighting the categories of functional work that appeared to evoke these challenges.[23]

We extend these earlier single-site analyses, using comparative case studies of three very different interventions to identify and analyze common issues, practices, and problems. We show that these issues, practices, and problems are not unique to individual interventions but are endemic to efforts to build and use educational infrastructure to change deeply rooted and unproductive practice in leadership, instruction, and student learning.

Currently, several interveners use the strategy of "improvement by design" to structure and manage a wide variety of school improvement networks, including those operated by comprehensive school reform providers, charter management organizations, and education management organizations. If we were to study these quite varied initiatives, one initial conjecture would be that their effectiveness would depend heavily on whether they could build their own versions of educational infrastructure to compensate for enduring weaknesses and incoherence in US education. To the extent that they took up that challenge, a corollary conjecture would be that they would encounter the puzzles of design, implementation, improvement, and sustainability that we discuss here, because they would face the same sort of complex interactions among their schools, designs, organizations, and environments that faced the three interventions that we studied.

One central thread in our analysis is that to appreciate the challenges that AC, ASP, and SFA encountered and the magnitude of their accomplishments, one must understand how their ambitious designs and novel organizations interacted with many weak schools, in environments that presented some assistance and many obstacles, during two decades. One reason that such work is poorly understood is that it is commonly thought to be comparatively straightforward and expeditious. For example, the architects of the New American Schools initiative assumed that initiatives such as America's Choice, Accelerated Schools, and Success for All could be brought to fruition in five to seven years by quickly shepherding interveners and schools through four clear and distinct phases: competition and selection; development; demonstration; and scale-up. Twenty years later, similar assumptions are evident in the three-phase structure of the federal Investing in Innovation (i3) program: development, validation, and scale-up.

We found no evidence that the work proceeds in accord with such assumptions. None. We are not alone. Our findings are consistent with other research on interventions that participated in New American Schools. They are consistent with research on franchise-like commercial replication that uses the same sort of hub-and-outlet structure of school improvement networks pursuing improvement by design. And they are consistent with leading comparative research on the emergence and maturation of innovations.[24]

Such work is more fruitfully framed not as an orderly progression from applied research to widespread utilization but as a collection of puzzles that can be understood and managed, but that often unfold in overlapping and nonsequential ways. To manage them is to untangle and manage complex interactions among schools, designs, and intervening organizations, and to do so in environments that are at least intermittently turbulent. Those interactions are the focus of our analysis.

TWO

The Design Puzzle

In common usage, "design" typically connotes a solution: a blueprint or sketch of how to transform an undesirable state of affairs into something better. For ASP, SFA, and AC, a fundamental puzzle was that their ambitions for developing new capabilities and coherence at scale precluded such a narrow conception. Rather, their ambitions required that they develop and manage comprehensive designs for improvement as they interacted with on-the-ground realities in the schools they sought to serve, the environments in which they sought to operate, and the organizations they were building to do the work.

This puzzle arose, in large measure, because ASP, SFA, and AC sought to improve capabilities and coherence in dysfunctional schools that operated in dysfunctional environments. These were schools and environments where existing capabilities and coherence were generally weak, particularly in the infrastructure needed to support high-quality instruction. This included weaknesses in school-level curriculum and assessments, opportunities for collaborative planning and instruction, and instructionally focused leadership. This also included weaknesses in broader educational infrastructure: for example, system-level standards and assessments, professional education for teachers and leaders, commercial instructional resources, and government-centered quality control and technical assistance.

Weaknesses in capabilities and coherence, in turn, interacted to undermine teaching and learning. For example, high-poverty schools often employed disproportionate numbers of poorly educated teachers, and they often lacked coordinated structures, roles, and resources to support their professional development. Consequent weaknesses in instruction often led to problems of student achievement, which reinforced low expectations for these students, which led to a dumbing down of academic content, which led to low achievement, and so on. Some "solutions" exacerbated these problems with voluminous, targeted, and uncoordinated innovations that did more to fragment schools than to provide coherent guidance for practice. Many were fielded by organizations that were likely to close up shop even before their programs could be abandoned by schools.

From the time of their founding through the late 1990s, all three interveners devised a distinct strategy for managing this puzzle: their own systems of solutions to the systems of problems that stood between the schools that existed and the schools they imagined. The three strategies bore resemblance to (and, in some cases, capitalized on) agendas for educational reform that had currency during the early to mid-1990s. They also reflected different ideas and philosophies of education reform, different understandings of systemic problems in schools and environments, and different experiences trying to solve those problems.

Consistent with principles of site-based management and professional community, ASP sought change in the culture and organization of schools, with the goal of developing capabilities in schools to design their own plans and methods for improving instruction. By contrast, SFA and AC targeted instruction directly with detailed designs for the work of students and teachers, and they developed new infrastructure to support designs for instruction. Even so, SFA and AC took different approaches. Tied tightly to Title I whole-school reform, SFA used a school-wide reading curriculum as its starting point. Tied tightly to the strengthening logic of standards-based reform, AC used academic standards and professional education as its starting points.

While these strategies increased possibilities for creating capabilities and coherence, they also left the interveners vulnerable. For example, one great question for ASP was whether weak schools could reinvent themselves systemically with such an open design, using change in culture and organization to improve academic work. The corresponding question for SFA and AC was whether weak schools could mobilize the knowledge and skill to use new infrastructure to support the intelligent and adaptive enactment of new designs for instruction. One great question for all three was whether they could accomplish such tasks while working from the outside in, as external partners lacking institutionalized funding and formal authority.

We begin to explore these matters here, with descriptive accounts of the strategies pursued by ASP, SFA, and AC as they evolved over the 1990s. We focus primarily on making clear how the interveners' strategies attended simultaneously to schools, their designs, their organizations, broader environments, and the relationships among them.[1] We do so for three reasons. The first is to scaffold readers into framing "design" not as a singular, point-in-time solution but, instead, as ongoing activity that attends to schools, designs, intervening organization, environments, and the relationships among them. The second is to provide necessary background and context that will support analyses in subsequent chapters. The third is to detail how confronting this essential design puzzle created vulnerabilities that arose from relationships among schools, their designs, their organizations, and broader environments. It was these vulnerabilities that the interveners needed to manage in moving their designs to practice.

Accelerated Schools

ASP: Core Strategy

The ASP strategy for building capabilities and coherence was to build a cultural foundation that would support schools in devising programs of instructional improvement responsive to their own students, teachers, and communities. These programs would span all grade levels and all content areas. As explained by ASP executives, "the goal of ASP is not to create identical replicas of one model across the country but to embed ASP in existing school cultures."[2]

To support cultural transformation, the Accelerated Schools Project began with a philosophy intended to serve as the primary organizer for school improvement efforts. The philosophy had three essential components: the belief that all students should be treated as gifted and talented; the ambition of powerful learning that would deeply engage all students in ambitious academic content; and a focus on strengths rather than deficits as the starting point for improvement. The philosophy was complemented by a multiyear process for applying and internalizing the philosophy that was anchored in participatory governance and management. Yet, as detailed by program developers, "the important changes . . . are not so much implementing the steps of the process as beginning an internal cultural transformation in the schools."[3]

Schools would enact the transformation process with assistance from agencies in their environments. Beyond supporting large-scale, school-level implementation, this was a deliberate effort to better integrate schools and existing agencies in their environments by establishing networks of like-minded organizations that embraced ASP's approach to improvement. That, in turn, increased prospects of sustainability by institutionalizing ASP's approach within the conventional, K–12 public education system. Near the end of ASP's first decade, ASP founder and Stanford University professor Henry Levin commented: "Our greatest success will be if this approach becomes so highly accepted in U.S. education that it does not need a label, but is the standard approach to educating children."[4]

The rationale for this strategy had three primary sources. The first was Levin's view that the key to accelerating the learning of at-risk students was academic enrichment (rather than remediation), and that implementing academic enrichment in schools required, above all, a strong cultural foundation. As Levin explained in a conference paper on the Accelerated Schools Project, "It is attitudes and modes of operation which are the greatest obstacles to change, not a lack of skills."[5] The second was the belief that, even if generally weak, both schools and environments were sources of untapped capabilities. The third was the belief that schools were likely to regard prescriptive, external improvement programs as bureaucratic directives at odds with strong traditions of local control and professional autonomy and thus resist them.

ASP: Schools

School-level problem solving was to be the core capability of ASP schools, from which would emerge interdependent improvements in philosophy, culture, and instruction. Hence, ASP sought to recruit schools that had at least some strength in domains that would directly support the program's approach to improvement. These would be schools that, despite their weaknesses, already believed that improvement began with cultural (rather than technical) transformation; that the knowledge, capabilities, and talent needed to improve were already in the building; and that family, community, and other proximal environments could function as resources for improvement. Their enlistment in ASP depended on a 90% vote for program adoption intended to affirm that schools shared ASP's vision and ambitions.

ASP's strategy for recruiting schools focused on establishing a system of satellite organizations that could work in partnership with a small, central ASP organization to support recruitment and implementation. (Both the central organization and the satellites are described in more detail below.) Again, rather than creating these satellite support centers from scratch, ASP sought to identify institutionalized educational organizations that shared an affinity for the ASP approach to improvement, were well established, and would use their own resources to advance ASP's cause.

With raw numbers of schools as the metric, this recruiting strategy was a success. ASP began in the early 1990s with a small number of schools, most in the San Francisco Bay area. By 2000, ASP's leaders estimated that it had expanded to a network of 1,400 schools. Beyond the initial pilot schools, most of this growth was through satellite affiliations with universities, colleges, state education agencies, and local school districts.

ASP: Design

ASP sought to build capabilities and coherence in these 1,400 schools. But again, the aim was not for one school improvement program to be replicated in 1,400 schools. Rather, it was for 1,400 unique school improvement programs, each devised locally and tailored to the strengths and needs of individual schools. These programs would all be based on a common philosophy, and they would be developed through a common process of cultural change.

Toward that end, the Accelerated Schools program sought to engage teachers and leaders in participative decision making that was anchored in the same sort of authentic inquiry that would drive powerful learning in classrooms.[6] Thus, direct teaching (via top-down leadership) was taboo. Rather, adult inquiry and learning would be active, inclusive, and "hands-on," featuring tasks that called for engaged reflection, dialogue, use of data, decision making, risk taking, invention, and application. As explained by ASP developers, "the kind of transformation we want children to make—to become active agents in their own learning—is very similar to the change we want school communities to make in their culture. In both cases, capacity to grow, to learn, and to succeed is being built."[7]

ASP's school-level design was comparatively loose on guidance for instruction, which was articulated as essential beliefs and norms (and not as specific practices). By contrast, it was comparatively tight on processes of school-level inquiry and decision making. The process was described as transformation: a school-wide effort to help teachers and school leaders learn to work together to realize more ambitious education by devising a vision and a strategic plan for their school's progress. While this expanded the scope of teachers' and leaders' work, it was held to be the key to cultural transformation.

The transformation process structured a series of collaborative tasks to be enacted in schools, with the intention of cultural change emerging and maturing from this work over a five-year period. These tasks included creating a vision; assessing current problems and strengths; setting priorities; solving problems; and making and implementing decisions. By enacting these tasks, schools would learn the ASP philosophy, come to understand powerful learning, and develop capability to act on that understanding. In 1998, ASP founder Henry Levin wrote that "as the school goes through each stage of the process, it builds capacity to implement powerful learning in which the values and principles of accelerated schools are embedded at all levels."[8] The process would change instruction by turning entire schools into more coherent and capable professional communities.

The Accelerated Schools program also specified school-level resources to support the enactment of these tasks. These resources included the elaboration of essential norms and values that would serve as a foundation for the transformation process: for example, viewing all students as gifted and talented, and developing powerful learning opportunities for them. They included three central principles to guide the enactment of the transformation process: unity of purpose, empowerment coupled with responsibility, and building on strengths. And they included organizational infrastructure to support the transformation process. This infrastructure began with a governance system featuring "cadres": small teams consisting of teachers, support staff, school leaders, parents, community members, and district personnel that would investigate specific priority problems in the school. A school-level "steering committee" consisting of cadre representatives would work centrally to keep the process on track and to coordinate the work. Finally, the School as a Whole (SAW) was to approve all decisions that had implications for the entire school.

Central to this organizational infrastructure were two new school leadership positions that, together, were critical to successful implementation: the external coach and the internal coach. Together, the external and internal coaches would design and offer training to orient school staff to each of the program's elements, offer ongoing encouragement, and troubleshoot. The external coach was to be a knowledgeable professional located in an agency in the environment of a particular ASP school who could offer external yet context-sensitive support. ASP encouraged schools to use local central office staff as external coaches, both to capital-ize on knowledge of local context and to embed the ASP philosophy and process in schools' proximal environments. Internal coaches were to be drawn from the school faculty, possibly with partial release from teach-ing responsibilities.

Consistent with ASP's commitment to decentralization, the actual selection of external and internal coaches was left to satellites and to schools, as was designing the work of coaches. For example, in selecting external coaches, some schools followed the general profile described above, whereas others used either satellite staff or made other provisions. For internal coaches, volunteers from a school would sometimes serve as internal coaches and not be released from teaching. External and in-ternal coaches then decided how to train teachers at their school, either by leveraging their own training from ASP satellites as a template or by customizing their own activities.

Tasks, norms, and organizational infrastructure were designed to in-teract, ultimately yielding not only change in culture but also increases in capabilities and coherence. Working as a community would help to improve and coordinate values and practices. With the transformation process building practice-based learning into the school's operations, teachers and school leaders would learn to be empowered and respon-sible, to work collaboratively, and to use the scientific method in the inquiry process to uncover problems and to generate solutions that em-bodied powerful learning. Leadership would thus be distributed across the school and unified by ASP's principles; it would not be concentrated in one person. From collaboration in a professional, inquiry-driven com-munity would emerge new capabilities, increased coherence, and shared understanding of (and commitment to) the ASP philosophy. If extended to instruction, these would function as a platform for powerful learning in classrooms.

In part due to a philosophical commitment not to provide schools and satellites with too-detailed guidance, ASP did not elaborate or formalize *instruction* using detailed routines and procedures. Instead, ASP elabo-rated the *transformation process* using routines and procedures, comple-mented by materials that used conversational prose to explain key ideas and to provide examples of their application. Such materials were used to explain the fundamental concept of powerful learning and the linkages between culture and instruction. Some materials were produced by ASP itself; others were produced by satellites and then vetted and redistrib-uted by ASP.

One cornerstone resource was the more than three-hundred-page *Accelerated Schools Resource Guide*, which discussed the overall philosophy of ASP and each element of the design.[9] Another cornerstone resource was an implementation assessment kit, which was intended to help schools and satellites to get an overview of schools' strengths and weaknesses and to build capability. In the late 1990s, the kit featured eighty-seven "Benchmarks for 'Demonstrated' Implementation" organized around three topics: powerful learning, the governance structure and process, and the ASP philosophy. ASP complemented these cornerstone resources with a thrice-yearly newsletter that dealt with such topics as building capability, assessing schools' progress, and powerful learning, along with a website that offered other materials that addressed such topics as the learning theories behind powerful learning, research results, and examples of school success. While no one was required to visit the site or read materials, ASP encouraged schools to do so.

Thus, rather than show teachers how to organize classrooms, how to set goals, how to diagnose student learning, or what texts to use, ASP sought to help schools and satellites to build the cultural foundation and organizational infrastructure that would enable schools to turn themselves into organizations that made their own good decisions about those things. This made the Accelerated Schools program seem much more open to many adopters either enthused about self-improvement and/or averse to more highly specified external intervention. It also was less expensive, in that it did not require extensive development capabilities within the ASP organization, nor did it require schools to purchase expensive curriculum materials (unless called for by their self-devised solutions).

This theory of improvement began with ASP's leaders. As ASP founder Henry Levin explained in a 1992 newsletter, "it is the implementation of the philosophy and principles that is the key to changing schools. It is a sad commentary that we have seen hundreds of schools across America with vision or mission statements on their walls, but without either vision or mission in their practices."[10] Gene Chasin, who eventually replaced Henry Levin as director of ASP, concurred. Summarizing ASP's theory of improvement in a 2007 interview, Chasin explained: "With cultural transformation, everyone in schools becomes the solution. Everyone becomes resourceful and focused. The centrality of inquiry toward the aim of equal opportunity for learning and growth transforms the way of looking at problems. It develops both instructional support elements and technical improvements based on the needs and strengths of each school."[11]

ASP: Organizations

Recognizing failures of many education reforms to provide substantial support for implementation, ASP's founders sought to support weak schools in enacting the process of cultural transformation. They did not choose to do so by developing a large, external organization that would assert centralized control. Rather, they sought to develop a strong but lean organization that would bring identity, coordination, and coherence to the effort. Indeed, the central ASP organization (called the National Center) would bring to the network exactly what the Accelerated Schools program brought to schools: unity of purpose, empowerment coupled with responsibility, and building on strength.

At its peak in 1994, the National Center consisted of approximately twelve full-time staff members and a similar number of part-time graduate students at Stanford University. One way that ASP's founders were able to limit the size of the National Center was by minimizing the need to develop, warehouse, and distribute extensive and detailed materials for schools and satellites. This was, in part, a matter of philosophical aversion to detailed guidance. But it was also pragmatic in that it meant that the National Center did not need to develop funding, staff, and capabilities to enact such work.

Another way that ASP's founders were able to limit the size of the National Center was through dependence on satellites to support recruitment and implementation. Indeed, the National Center saw its chief role as disseminating expertise away from the National Center by building capacity in satellites to support a national school improvement movement.[12] The National Center emphasized intellectual and strategic leadership. It aimed to train new satellite centers in the school design, to assist with their start-up, and to cultivate a shared sense of mission.

This was, again, due to ASP's philosophical commitment to empowering people and organizations in order to build on their strengths. But in the face of scarce resources, it would also have been difficult to construct a nationwide infrastructure to provide deep, sustained, and labor-intensive support for implementation under the umbrella of a research university.

ASP: Environments

Even though ASP believed that schools had strengths within, and even though ASP sought to provide some assistance through its National Center, its founders and developers also realized that success depended on schools leveraging resources in their environments. In a 2004 interview, when asked about the primary resource for new knowledge and capabilities for ASP teachers, one National Center executive responded that, rather than finding it in one place, teachers are "able to find the resources either within their colleagues or in their environment, at their colleges or professional development, through the district, or through reading."[13]

The success of ASP depended on schools identifying resources to support their self-constructed programs of improvement. Though ASP delegated to weak schools a great deal of instructional development work, the expectation was not that every school would reinvent the wheel. Rather, ASP's designers argued that schools could do this work because many instructional solutions—curricula, approaches to professional education, and the like—were available in the environment and could be used in ways consistent with ASP's values. Because cultural change was its engine, the ASP design could fit with varied curricula, standards, and circumstances, as long as they were philosophically congruent. In a 1994 newsletter, ASP reported:

Members of Accelerated School communities take special care to ensure packages or programs support the school's identified needs and vision. Using the Accelerated Schools philosophy and process, the school shapes the program so that it builds on the Accelerated Schools powerful learning approach . . . and meets [the school's] unique needs. . . . [Such] packages or programs have much more meaning in an Accelerated School because they are implemented within the school's changing culture and not in isolation of one another.[14]

As described above, the success of ASP also depended on a system of satellite organizations that could work in partnership both to recruit schools and to support the enactment of the transformation process. By 2000, ASP had succeeded in establishing partnership agreements with eleven satellite organizations.

ASP's partnership agreements specified a small set of consistent training structures, days, and topics for schools that would be provided over a three-year contract, a period that squared with the three years of school-level funding available under the federal Obey-Porter Comprehensive School Reform Demonstration Act of 1997. The general model began with regional training sessions for school leaders provided by senior satellite staff. It continued with satellite staff visiting schools at least three times per year to track the transformation process, provide support, consult, and troubleshoot. While satellite staff set details, school visits typically combined classroom observation with meetings with school leaders, steering committees, and even entire schools. Regional network meetings and an annual national conference provided additional opportunities for coaches, principals, and teachers to meet with their counterparts in other schools and to attend workshops and training sessions.

Yet the partnership agreement with satellites was at least as much covenant as contract. Satellites were expected to embrace ASP's vision, philosophy, and transformation process. Reciprocally, ASP afforded satellites considerable discretion in the design and enactment of their work. In keeping with ASP's belief in existing capabilities and its commitment to decentralization, satellites were to be empowered but responsible, with the combination intended to encourage ownership and motivation. Training was intended to vary across satellites, with quality control dependent on the dedication of satellite staff and the cultural identity of the movement. As such, satellites were expected to address a common set of core topics (e.g., powerful learning, building on strengths, and collaborative inquiry) by creating or borrowing curricula and other resources to customize their assistance.

This system of satellites grew in lockstep with the installed base of schools. Again, ASP's National Center at Stanford University was the initial source of support for schools. Beyond that, the next four satellites were launched in 1990 in four states, funded by a corporate grant. By 1992, there were ten satellites and a state education agency–led network of schools in another state.[15] After funding the first satellites, Levin decided that they should be financially independent, which he saw as consistent with ASP's principles of local empowerment coupled with responsibility. As explained by ASP leaders, "the National Center considers satellite centers to be collegial institutions which contribute to the development of the model, help disseminate new practices and research, and share local innovations with the nationwide network of centers and schools."[16]

During the 1990s, the establishment of the National Center, the satellites, and their relationships was a work in progress. Beginning in 1996, the National Center began to shift its organization and funding. It set up a National Policy Advisory Board composed of satellite and National Center leaders. It sought to collect a fee from each satellite, prorated by the number of schools in the satellite network, so that the National Center's funding would not depend entirely on grants. This was the beginning of efforts to exert somewhat greater central control—efforts that would intensify in later years. The National Center also sought to build on the strengths of its organization's emerging identity as a movement.

Through the 1990s, leaders in satellites and the National Center collaborated to create and implement new resources that would be used at the
discretion of satellites and schools, an example of the distributed leadership that ASP urged for schools.

Thus, ASP's strategy depended on weak schools taking crucial steps to
turn themselves from the problem into its solution. But to solve the problem of what it called ownership, ASP delegated a great deal of the redesign
of instruction to schools, requiring weak organizations to devise or com-
pose academically ambitious instruction that they never had known, in
collaboration with external agencies learning to do much the same. What
then became "ASP" in a given school was only loosely constrained by the
National Center, primarily via the articulation of norms and values and
the elaboration of the transformation process. What became ASP varied
intentionally with each and every ASP school. Working within ASP's system of beliefs, there was really no other way.

Success for All

SFA: Core Strategy

Where ASP sought to improve instruction by changing culture, SFA
sought to change culture by improving instruction. Specifically, SFA
sought to use tested routines embedded in detailed curriculum materials
to effect a quick change in teachers' work. That, in turn, would enable
at-risk students to succeed, with their success then initiating an upward,
school-wide spiral of enthusiasm, commitment, and improvement.

Moreover, where ASP deferred primary responsibility for program development to schools and their environments, SFA located primary responsibility for program development in the central organization itself.
Again, the heart of SFA's strategy for school improvement was a centrally
developed design for instruction. The instructional design, then, was
embedded in a comprehensive, school-wide reading curriculum which,
in turn, was embedded within a centrally developed design for school
organization.

Rather than norms and values as a beginning point (as with ASP),
SFA began with targets and goals. Specifically, SFA targeted K–6 reading
instruction in underperforming schools, with the goal of all students (especially at-risk students) reading at grade level at the end of each grade.

SFA's cofounders saw reading instruction as the core responsibility and capability of elementary schools, and they saw failure in early reading as producing lifelong consequences for students. Thus, with its primary focus on K–6 reading, SFA developers sought to make their program the core, standard operating procedure in schools.

Differences between ASP and SFA arose in part from different assumptions about the capabilities and coherence of schools and their environments. ASP's founders saw enough strength in targeted schools and environments to begin school-based efforts to develop instructional improvement programs. By contrast, SFA's founders saw enough weaknesses to undermine such work. The differences also arose from different understandings about detailed, external guidance for school improvement. ASP's founders saw such guidance as usurping local control and initiative. By contrast, SFA's cofounders saw detailed, external guidance as enabling schools to do much more for students than they would have otherwise, primarily by increasing capabilities and coherence through the replication of research-based, research-proven, and experience-refined practices.

SFA: Schools

Where ASP and SFA both targeted schools with large numbers of at-risk students, SFA focused more narrowly on schools eligible to use federal Title I funding to support school-wide improvement. In fact, SFA intentionally structured costs so that the program would be affordable for Title I schools, in part as a strategic effort to stabilize the program by linking it to an institutionalized funding stream.

Like ASP, SFA sought to use recruitment and selection of schools to identify schools that were knowledgeable about (and disposed to) SFA's technically focused strategy for improvement. To do so, SFA specified a program adoption process that required a regimen of program awareness activities, followed by an 80% vote for adoption by the school's instructional staff.

Once recruited, SFA sought to link schools into local and national networks, with the central SFA organization functioning as the coordinating hub of the networks. These networks would function as a sort of "alternative system" in which schools could collaborate to support their use of the design. Developing such a network was a goal that dated to SFA's earliest days at Johns Hopkins University. As argued by program developers, "systemic and lasting change is far more likely when schools work together as part of a network in which school staff share a common vision and a common language, share ideas and technical assistance, and create an emotional connection and support system."[17]

SFA's recruiting strategy was a success. Between 1987/88 and 2000/1, the SFA enterprise expanded from a single school in Baltimore to 1,600 schools distributed across the country. This rapid increase to a state-sized network of schools was enabled not only by federal Title I funding but also by support from the New American Schools initiative, the federal Obey-Porter Comprehensive School Reform Demonstration Act of 1997, the federal Reading Excellence Act of 1998, and numerous state and district initiatives that supported comprehensive school reform (some of which identified SFA as an approved—and sometimes favored—provider).

SFA: Design

Rather than focusing on a process of collaborative inquiry among adults, the Success for All program centered on a process of classroom instruction among students and teachers. While Success for All was a comprehensive school reform program, the heart of that program was a specific design for instruction. From there, Success for All worked backward to a coordinated, school-wide curriculum and, from there, to the organizational resources and professional principles needed to support implementation.

The Success for All instructional design was constructed around a "cycle of diagnostic instruction" that combined direct instruction, cooperative learning, individual assessment, and celebration of success, all focused on skills and strategies students needed to decode and make meaning of texts. Students were to practice using reading skills and strategies in cooperative learning teams, on the argument that collaboration among students both supported student achievement and developed positive social relationships. Teachers were to provide direct instruction in reading skills and strategies and to model their use. Central to the teacher role was observing students' efforts to use reading skills and strategies in cooperative learning teams, assessing their progress, diagnosing problems, and providing immediate remedial support.[18]

To support enactment of the instructional design, SFA developers drew on research and experience to develop formal, codified instructional routines, ranging from step-by-step directions to frameworks that structured classroom-specific planning. Routines were complemented with assessments, forms, and other information resources to support instructional decision making, as well as by supplemental guidance that provided additional information about the rationale and enactment of the instructional design.

Routines, information resources, and supplemental guidance were embedded in conventional curriculum materials and other resources that could be reproduced quickly, purchased by schools, and distributed rapidly. Moreover, the curriculum materials were formatted and specified at a level intended to enable weak teachers both to use them quickly and effectively at a base level with only a minimum of support and, with accumulating experience and capabilities, to use them more flexibly in addressing the needs of students.

In contrast to Accelerated Schools and America's Choice, Success for All included a complete K–6 reading curriculum intended to bring school-wide coherence to instruction. It could fairly be seen as a package of ready-to-use practices that had demonstrated effects, had been replicated across schools, and had been refined over time with experience. The curriculum was extensive, including detailed schedules and pacing guides, scripts to guide some parts of direct instruction, detailed frameworks within which to plan other parts, detailed learning tasks for students to perform in cooperative teams, standard work products and assessments, and standardized record keeping and reporting.

Success for All specified an aggressive (though developmentally sensitive) implementation sequence that spanned three years. Implementation would begin school-wide on Day 1 of Year 1 as an SFA school. One first-year goal was faithful enactment of research-based and experience-refined classroom practices, with the potential for early, positive effects on student achievement and, with that, positive effects on teachers' expectations of students and their responsibility for improvement. Another goal was to build instructional coherence anchored in a language of instruction shared by all teachers, in valid and reliable information on which to base diagnoses of students' problems, and in shared knowledge and experience in which to anchor interpretation of information. For the second and third years, as both capabilities and coherence increased, the goals changed to working flexibly and adaptively within the program, with teachers using new routines, information resources, and guidance to identify and address students' academic and nonacademic needs.

Beyond the reading curriculum, Success for All included organizational infrastructure to support the work of students and teachers, with the twin goals of improving capabilities among teachers and coherence across schools. For example, Success for All provided guidance for creating a ninety-minute, school-wide reading block, which was intended both to increase instructional time and to reduce class size by assigning all available teachers to teach reading. Success for All provided routines and assessments for regrouping students across grade levels each quarter based on their reading performance, so that teachers could focus on narrower bands of students. These resources went further, to include tutoring and family support teams to assist the most struggling students; "component teams" to support collaborative learning among teachers; and routines for attendance management, classroom management, and conflict resolution among students.

Paralleling ASP's coaches, Success for All also created a leadership team with responsibility for school-wide implementation and effectiveness. The leadership team was headed by the reading facilitator, a newly created leadership role. Described as "the linchpin of the program," the reading facilitator would ideally be a lead teacher with unusual capability to support students and teachers. Combined with the requirement of an 80% vote for program adoption by instructional staff, the intention was for Success for All to be both a *teacher-selected* and *teacher-led* program. While broadly responsible for implementation and effectiveness, chief among the responsibilities of the reading facilitator was conveying, modeling, and scaffolding adaptive, locally responsive use of the program. As described in the Success for All *Facilitator's Manual*, the primary print resource provided by SFA to school leaders,

This program works best in the hands of competent teachers challenged to use their own professional judgment in deciding many important questions about implementation. As the facilitator, you must model the use of good judgment. Nothing this or any manual could possibly include eliminates the need for you to consult with teachers often, to weigh facts carefully, to read relevant research reports and review the principles embedded in the program, and to make your own, sound professional decisions. Effective implementation depends on your reflective and adaptive leadership.[19]

Alongside its extensive curriculum materials and organizational infrastructure, a core commitment of SFA was to provide school-based support for implementation. Prior to implementation, SFA trainers taught teachers and school leaders how to begin enacting the program on Day 1 of Year 1 as a Success for All school. Thereafter, SFA trainers primarily sought to develop capabilities in school leaders to support teachers' practice-based learning. This assistance came in the form of direct instruction during national conferences, modeling essential instructional and leadership practices during school-based implementation visits (typically eight to twelve days per year), and direct instruction during optional training modules for which schools could contract.

All of this work was to be driven by three "first principles" of practice in all SFA schools: prevention, early intervention, and relentlessness. Prevention meant using research-based practices to keep achievement problems from occurring in the first place. Early intervention meant aggressive, targeted, and coherent use of research-based and experience-refined practices at the first sign of learning problems in regular classroom instruction, tutoring, and family support. Relentlessness meant continuously adapting instructional and other services to address students' academic and nonacademic needs. As explained by Success for All's designers, "success does not come from piling on additional services but from coordinating human resources around a well-defined goal, constantly assessing progress towards that goal, and never giving up until success is achieved."[20]

SFA: Organizations

Just as SFA's design contrasted strongly with ASP's, so too did its central organization. Over its first decade, SFA's central organization evolved from a ten-person project team at Johns Hopkins University to the independent, nonprofit Success for All Foundation (SFAF), with 250 staff members based at its headquarters in Towson, MD, and with another 250 in a nationally distributed, regionally structured training organization. This was a complex organization formally organized into divisions and departments with capabilities for research, development, training, business operations, conference and travel planning, materials production and distribution, and more. In addition to its comprehensive school reform program, the organization also supported programs in other content areas and levels of schooling. Even with increasing size, complexity, and formalization, members reported that the organization maintained a mission-driven culture, strong social relationships among staff members, and norms of continuous learning and improvement that had roots in its founding as an academic research and development center.

Growth in the enterprise brought with it a need for more highly developed executive capabilities. Yet SFAF neither recruited executives from the business sector nor developed executive staff functions (e.g., marketing, lobbying, and policy analysis). Rather, SFAF continued to be led by Robert Slavin and Nancy Madden, the husband-and-wife team that cofounded Success for All. Themselves experienced researchers and developers, Slavin and Madden were assisted by long-serving colleagues with similar capabilities. The leadership of Slavin and Madden was instrumental in maintaining SFAF's mission-driven character and its strong social relationships. Indeed, staff members referred to SFAF as one big "mom-and-pop shop."

This large, complex organization emerged, in part, from needs that arose from SFA's core commitments to mine research, produce materials, support their use, evaluate effects on practice and outcomes, and continuously improve. It also emerged as a consequence of its environments. In an effort to reduce demands on the organization by leveraging available resources, SFA's founders and developers sought to mine environments for curriculum, assessments, and other essential resources. Moreover, they also sought to collaborate with external development, training, and research partners to reduce demands on the organization. Even so, they experienced educational environments quite differently from ASP's founders and developers. Specifically, they found very few high-quality resources that they could readily incorporate and immediately use, and they found external partnerships difficult to establish and manage. Indeed, even with its commitments to use research as the basis for its design, SFA was forced to compensate for weaknesses in the available research base by developing extensive capabilities for experiential learning in collaboration with schools.

Of all the environmental resources that were in short supply, two headed the list. One was a ready supply of capable experts who could staff SFA's training organization. While SFA provided extensive resources to support implementation, capabilities and coherence would increase only if teachers and school leaders learned to use new resources to work in new ways. Yet, absent a ready labor pool in environments, SFA had to hire and develop trainers who could support all of this learning.

The other resource in short supply was money. To build such a complex enterprise on a large scale required capital well beyond what it took to simply develop the program. Materials had to be designed, printed, and distributed, and trainers had to be recruited, equipped, and educated. These were not small costs. Printing costs exceeded $20 million annually, and recruiting, equipping, and educating just one trainer cost roughly $50,000.[21] This was all cash-out-of-pocket before billing schools. On the one hand, operating as a nonprofit, SFA struggled to secure operating capital from external funders. On the other hand, its founders believed that it would not be viable to raise capital by becoming a for-profit organization and soliciting investors. They worried that doing so would confound the mission of serving at-risk students with the complex incentives of for-profit organizations.

Operating as a nonprofit foundation, SFAF devised a complex funding scheme that was intended to respond both to the organization's resource needs and to environmental opportunities and constraints. Development and research were funded by public and private contributions, buoyed by the dot-com boom of the 1990s. Training was an independent, fee-for-service organization. Again, securing operating capital for the central organization was difficult. When it was originally founded, SFAF lacked assets. To compensate, it secured loans from philanthropists against which it established a line of credit. That became SFAF's chief operating capital, complemented by the sale of materials to schools and revenues from training. All were weighted heavily toward first year schools that purchased a full complement of materials and training in Year 1. With that, continued scale-up was not only central to SFAF's mission to reach as many at-risk students as possible. It was also key to maintaining its cash flow.

Thus, while ASP's strategy for improvement *created* extensive demands on environments for technical resources and satellite partners, SFA's strategy was intended to *reduce* demands on environments for the resources and personnel needed to support large-scale instructional improvement. The trade-off, though, was the need to establish a much more complex central organization. SFA had many more responsibilities than did ASP's National Center, including the development of materials, the recruitment and education of trainers, and the production of knowledge needed to support its efforts. In some ways, this yielded benefits in economies of scale. With design responsibilities centralized, schools would be freed to attend to implementation. Yet it also brought real costs. Developing and supporting the program in many weak schools required developing complex capabilities in the central organization, and that required time, effort, and money.

SFA: Environments

Even though SFA sought to reduce its dependence on environments, it still relied on them for the legitimacy, funding, and stability needed to construct and operate the enterprise. SFA sought to manage and mediate environments to achieve these ends.

SFA began by aligning and realigning its school-level design to maintain its currency amid changing federal and state policies. For example,

SFA structured the costs of its school-level design such that high-poverty schools could purchase the program with Title I funds, sometimes complemented by other funds of the same sort. The design also was crafted to fit within the parameters of the New American Schools initiative and then recrafted to fit the parameters of key federal policies: for example, successive reauthorizations of the Elementary and Secondary Education Act (in which resided Title I); the Obey-Porter Comprehensive School Reform Demonstration Act of 1997; and the Reading Excellence Act of 1998.

SFA also sought to influence policy environments through aggressive lobbying and advocacy. To increase the appeal and legitimacy of Success for All in policy environments that appeared to place an increasing premium on effectiveness, developers anchored the program in research, validated it with studies of its effects, and promoted Success for All as showing positive program effects. It urged states to allocate funds to support schools' adoption of Success for All, and it used reports on the performance of SFA schools on state accountability assessments as further evidence of program effectiveness. It also urged federal support for school-wide, research-based improvement.

Beyond aligning with (and attempting to influence) policy, SFA also sought to manage schools' relationships with their environments to support work at scale. For example, as a part of the initial program adoption process, SFA contracted with district central offices to secure support, to exempt its schools from some district requirements, and to insulate them from local practices that might disrupt implementation. Beyond that, the Success for All program included a key component—family support—charged with maintaining relationships with parents and community organizations.

SFA's efforts to manage and mediate environments doubled back onto its organization, design, and schools. SFA developed informal capabilities to constantly monitor environments for problems, expectations, resources, and opportunities. Beyond supporting strategic management, information generated via this monitoring also drove the continuous adaptation and evolution of the program.

Thus, by 2000/1, SFA had evolved into a comprehensive, complex design for schools, a large, complex central organization, a network with more than a thousand schools, all in complex relations with environments. Yet success depended on the Success for All program making its way into dysfunctional schools and environments without systemic dysfunction making its way into the program. The program and its associated supports for implementation would have to be interpreted as resources for professional practice, problem solving, and learning, and not as bureaucratic, top-down directives or as technocratic quick fixes. For this to happen, school leaders would have to quickly develop the capability to assist teachers in using program resources both faithfully and adaptively. At the same time, SFA would have to develop schools' capability to exploit local and national networks to improve implementation, and it would have to develop schools' capabilities both to buffer and to leverage environmental resources to support implementation. To do these things, SFA would have to produce materials, recruit and develop trainers, manage effectively at scale, develop executive capability, and raise more money. The success of all this was predicated on securing legitimacy, funding, and stability in notoriously turbulent environments.

America's Choice

AC: Core Strategy

Where ASP led with culture and SFA with curriculum, AC's core strategy led with professional education. AC sought to support teachers in using their professional knowledge to design and enact instruction that was both responsive to the immediate needs of students and coordinated across classrooms. Yet doing so required devising and enacting professional learning opportunities through which teachers would develop that professional knowledge and learn to use it in practice. In that sense, AC aimed to be a highly mobile teacher education program with the capacity to work from coast to coast.

Thus, responsibility for designing and enacting high-quality instruction was shared by the AC organization and by teachers. These efforts depended on three key resources. The first was ambitious performance standards and common reference exams that established shared goals for mastering reading, writing, and mathematics. The second was a set of instructional frameworks intended to support and coordinate teachers in developing and enacting learning opportunities tailored to the needs of their students. The third was an ethos of professionalism that privileged teachers, their knowledge, and their expertise as the chief levers for improving student achievement. AC's developers saw these resources as instrumental in supporting large-scale, sustainable operations by institutionalizing high-quality instruction once AC no longer directly supported the day-to-day work of schools.

AC devised this strategy because the experiences of its founders and initial developers convinced them that teachers were unlikely to have the professional knowledge needed to design and enact ambitious classroom instruction. They also believed that providing only broad principles of instruction (as in ASP) was unlikely to help teachers move beyond established practice. AC's founders and initial developers saw one root cause of teachers' weaknesses as educational environments that set weak standards for student performance. They saw another as a teaching profession that lacked knowledge of effective instructional practice and high-quality professional education for teachers. However, AC's founders and initial developers also believed that academically ambitious instruction could not be built around prescribed practice and materials (as in SFA). Hence they sought to create a program that would privilege the professional education, knowledge, and autonomy of teachers.[22]

AC: Schools

Like ASP and SFA, AC sought to improve education for large numbers of at-risk students by organizing a large number of schools as a professional network. As explained by Marc Tucker, founder of AC and its parent organization, the National Center on Education and the Economy (NCEE), "the issue was to change the system and how to work at scale. That was always the issue. So, from my point of view, if we didn't find a way to solve the [scale] problem, we failed."[23]

Developing its own professional network of schools had not always been NCEE's strategy. Indeed, as a predecessor to AC, NCEE had initiated an effort called the National Alliance for Restructuring Education in 1989, which had NCEE collaborating with states and districts to develop capabilities and coherence within the institutionalized system of K–12 public education. As reported by Tucker, "It was a dismal failure. The scope of the problem was much too large in relation to the amount of resources at our disposal."[24]

With the decision to instead pursue large-scale change through comprehensive school reform, AC began with the same strategy as ASP and AC: it recruited schools predisposed to its core strategy for improvement. In the case of AC, this meant recruiting schools that were among the first in the country to acknowledge the need to develop capabilities that would allow them to work within a system of standards and assessments to improve student achievement.

Leveraging its participation in the New American Schools initiative, AC's recruiting strategy initially worked school by school to secure commitment to AC. In its first year of operations in 1999, this strategy proved successful, with forty-five schools signing on as the first cohort of AC schools. As detailed in chapter 4, AC would soon shift its recruiting strategy, and it would soon experience a twelve-fold increase in the number of schools in its network. However, in the late 1990s, when a decade of activity by ASP and SFA had already resulted in state-sized networks of schools, AC's initial launch in 1999 had it working with a district-sized network of schools.

AC: Design

To support these schools, AC developed a design that was predicated first and foremost on an analysis of environmental deficits: specifically, analyses suggesting that US educational environments lacked key features of educational infrastructure common in many other countries. Analyses of environmental deficits, in turn, drove the design for comprehensive school reform to compensate for those deficits.

The America's Choice instructional design consisted of three key components: coordinated performance standards and reference exams; guidance for planning and enacting ambitious academic instruction; and organizational infrastructure to support teachers in developing the knowledge and capabilities to make effective use of performance standards and instructional guidance.

Performance standards and reference exams were by far the most detailed parts of the instructional design. The performance standards specified in detail what students should know and how they should demonstrate mastery in reading, writing, and mathematics for grades 4, 8, and 10. Reference exams specified in detail exactly how mastery would be measured.

AC saw performance standards and reference exams as a basis for instructional focus and coherence, for coordination among teachers, and for a school culture that valued rigorous learning for all students. Rather than each teacher interpreting goals and measuring success individually, developers reasoned that performance standards and coordinated reference exams would establish common goals as the basis for comparison and joint work. As explained by Phil Daro, director of curriculum and one of the original architects of the America's Choice program, "the point is that these are standards-based classrooms. Everyone knows what the standards are and what they have to do to meet them."[25]

Like ASP and SFA, AC depended heavily on materials to convey standards and assessments to schools: it produced a multivolume collection of resources that detailed what students were to learn, provided extensive samples of student work at different stages of development, and more. The performance standards had been devised from scratch, in collaboration with the New Standards Project within the Learning Research and Development Center at the University of Pittsburgh. Though the product of a long-term, multimillion dollar development effort, the standards were easily reproduced and transported once created. By the late 1990s, over ten thousand copies had been sold to schools.[26]

America's Choice complemented standards and reference exams with instructional guidance intended to support teachers in developing lessons and academic tasks that addressed students' needs, that were aligned with the standards, and that were coordinated across classrooms. Instructional guidance in America's Choice was neither as loose as in Accelerated Schools nor as tight as in Success for All. Instead, America's Choice provided instructional frameworks that guided teachers in planning for and designing instruction in common, coherent ways. Called Readers and Writers Workshops, the guidance included templates for constructing lessons, processes for grouping students, techniques for assessing progress, guidance for allocating time, and criteria for selecting and using texts. While detailed, this guidance still allowed teachers considerable discretion in designing and enacting classroom instruction in ways responsive to students' evolving needs.[27] As Daro explained, "in this system, teachers need to know where kids are all the time. There's constant monitoring and constant regrouping. Kids are grouped by their level of performance but the groups are constantly re-done."[28]

Though less detailed than the standards, the instructional frameworks also were represented in material resources, with the intent of formalizing expert knowledge of teaching and learning. Rather than designed from scratch, the instructional frameworks drew on existing models. Specifically, Writers Workshop was based on the work of Lucy Calkins and Donald Graves, and Readers Workshop leaned heavily on both Reading Recovery and Gay Su Pinnel's work in guided reading. Both had achieved a level of visibility and recognition among education reformers, and both had research showing evidence of effectiveness.

Unlike Success for All, the America's Choice standards, assessments, and frameworks were not designed to be used immediately and effectively with existing knowledge and expertise. Rather, the America's Choice materials required that teachers learn how to transform content standards into fruitful lessons for many different students.[29] Moreover, they needed to learn to do so consistently, within the America's Choice instructional frameworks. Doing all of this at scale, in turn, required that AC developers create opportunities for thousands of what they saw as modestly educated teachers in weak schools to learn how to use AC-provided resources to devise new curriculum and new teaching practices. This was a tall order, requiring that teachers have knowledge of standards, performance assessments, instructional grouping, text analysis, instructional differentiation, and more.[30] Absent such knowledge, AC developers were concerned that teachers were apt either to make poor instructional decisions or to revert to past practice.

A first step toward building this knowledge was to establish shared norms and values that would serve as a cultural foundation for improvement. The norms and values began with the performance standards, which articulated expectations for student performance that teachers and leaders were to internalize and for which they would assume responsibility. These norms and values went further, to include a strong emphasis on the professional status of teachers. AC developers believed that, by providing teachers with authentic learning opportunities that were tied to practice and that enabled them to work more effectively with students, teachers would be more likely to embrace the program. As explained by AC executive and developer Judy Codding, "teachers see us as having them do more professional work. They recognize that."[31]

America's Choice went further by including a design for organizational infrastructure to support teachers in building fundamental knowledge of reading, writing, instruction, texts, and standards that could then be brought to bear on the design and enactment of instruction. With this infrastructure, one goal was to anchor teachers' professional learning in their daily practice, such that teachers would be immediately able to try out new ideas and to receive instant feedback. A second goal was to create extended time and opportunity for teachers' learning under the supervision of an AC-provided demonstration teacher. A third goal was to support ambitions for large-scale operations. As explained by Daro, "in our schools, the demonstration teacher is in the school over a period of years. Staff development is based in schools. It's about implementation, not workshops. Teachers learn something and then go immediately to try it in their classrooms."[32]

The organizational infrastructure within America's Choice included formal structures intended to turn schools into centers of professional learning, to help educators to learn radically different practices, and to enhance schools' coherence and capability. Chief among these structures was the creation of a "model classroom" in which teachers could observe high-quality implementation of the classroom model. As explained by AC developers:

The literacy teacher, who has been released from having her own classes, finds a sympathetic and good first-grade teacher who will be willing to let her work with her class. The literacy teacher practices the model on this class for maybe half a year. After she has learned it, she begins to model it for other teachers. She does this by modeling it in each teacher's classroom. After she finishes the first grade she moves on to the second grade.[33]

The organizational infrastructure of America's Choice also included two new leadership roles that would be drawn from the school's faculty and that would lead instructional improvement: the design coach and the literacy coordinator.[34] Just as in ASP and SFA, these new leadership roles were the linchpins of effective, school-level implementation. More than anyone else, the design coach and the literacy coordinator were charged with using AC-provided resources as a springboard for improving teacher capability and instruction. They had the lion's share of responsibility for training teachers, monitoring instruction, collaborating with teachers to solve instructional problems, and building norms and capabilities for the professional discourse that would support such collaboration. They also served as the primary liaisons with the central AC organization.

Design coaches and literacy coordinators were themselves the targets of intensive professional development: three to four weeks of training from AC staff members per year, complemented by annual conferences, workshops, and training sessions that they attended with their principals and their counterparts from other schools. After all, with leadership roles thus constructed, the resulting knowledge demands on the design coach and the literacy coordinator actually exceeded those on teachers. School leaders needed knowledge of standards, performance assessment, instructional grouping, text analysis, and instructional differentiation. But they also needed capabilities to represent and model the complex practices manifest in the instructional design, to assess teachers' understandings and enactment of the instructional design, to develop professional learning opportunities responsive to teachers' needs, and to surface and manage resistance among teachers.

Though schools were under pressure to improve quickly, America's Choice deliberately structured a more measured rollout within schools. Where the detailed elaboration of practice in Success for All enabled schools to begin school-wide implementation on Day 1 of Year 1 as an SFA school, America's Choice was designed to roll out implementation one teacher at a time, with the model classroom functioning as the primary venue within which individual teachers developed the professional knowledge and expertise needed to successfully enact the instructional design. Even if work in the model classroom went well, progress would be slow, possibly taking more than one academic year to achieve coordinated, school-wide implementation.

AC: Organizations

With their design, AC developers took deliberate efforts to mitigate demands on their own organization: for example, by developing the America's Choice standards in collaboration with the Learning Research and Development Center at the University of Pittsburgh; by incorporating existing instructional designs with Readers Workshop and Writers Workshop; and by seeking to develop school-based capacity to support teachers' professional learning. Even so, perceived weaknesses in environments interacted with developers' ambitions for schools to create the need for a large and capacious central organization.

When AC was launched in 1998, the central organization employed about a hundred people in Washington, DC, Fort Worth, Texas, and Oakland, California. Much like SFA, AC's central organization would soon evolve to include capabilities for program development, training, quality control, and executive leadership. Most critical was AC's field-based training organization, which was responsible for developing in teachers and school leaders the knowledge needed to successfully enact the instructional design.

The training organization included two key roles: AC cluster leaders and AC coaches (as distinct from design coaches in schools). AC cluster leaders and AC coaches were responsible for providing eight days of practice-based support in schools every year. This support included visiting classes, helping design coaches and literacy coordinators assess needs, meeting with school leaders to plan next steps, and, in some cases, modeling instructional practices. They were also responsible for the additional three to four weeks of professional development for design coaches and literacy coordinators.

As a consequence, AC had to recruit staff members who could, in turn, recruit and train AC coaches and cluster leaders. Though AC tried to recruit talented individuals to work as coaches and cluster leaders, new recruits still had to learn the America's Choice design, the underlying ideas about teaching and learning, the change process in schools, reading instruction, writing instruction, leadership, and more. These coaches and cluster leaders would then develop new knowledge and capabilities in school-level design coaches and literacy coordinators. Working in collaboration with AC coaches and cluster leaders, the school-level design coaches and literacy coordinators would then develop the knowledge and capabilities in teachers to support successful enactment of the instructional design.

These demands were initially manageable. In 1999 AC was still relatively small, with a network of forty-five schools. Much of the work of recruiting and developing field-based training staff could be done by AC's original leaders and developers. This was a knowledgeable and seasoned group, with experience as teachers and principals, as leaders of state-level instructional improvement initiatives, and as participants in international instructional improvement initiatives.[35]

In the early years, many of these people played multiple roles, which eased some problems of coordination and capability within AC's own organization. Program developers who spent most of their time creating new materials also trained coaches and visited schools. Even top staffers worked directly with schools, thus reducing the need to train others to support implementation. Organizational problems could be worked out informally, and information was easily exchanged. Top staff could closely follow implementation in schools and monitor their performance.

But as AC began to grow, so did the organization and the associated costs. Geographically dispersed schools, a design that required intensive professional learning, and a relatively small central organization meant that staff spent a great deal of time traveling. Consequently, the organization operated at a frenzied pace.[36]

The breadth of AC's activities increased these costs. In addition to the elementary school design discussed here, AC developed middle and high school programs as well as a school-to-work transition program. The array continued to grow through the first years, with many new programs and initiatives. In connection with this diversification, the organization incorporated business expertise, hiring, for example, the former manager of a high-tech start-up to oversee sales and marketing. This habit later became more pronounced, just as it would in SFA.

AC: Environments

All of the preceding led to complex relationships between AC and its environments. The entire enterprise was predicated on analyses and experiences that led AC's founders and initial developers to the conclusion that US education environments were deficient in key system-level infrastructure. Despite those deficits and attempts to compensate, AC still remained dependent on its environments, and for the same three things as SFA: legitimacy, resources, and stability. AC's leaders worked hard to secure all three.

In terms of legitimacy and resources, AC's leaders aggressively pursued foundation grants to support the development of new materials and programs, the cost of which was not covered by fees from schools. In the late 1990s economic boom, Marc Tucker first secured funds from New American Schools initiative. Subsequent grants from the Pew Charitable Trust and the MacArthur Foundation provided development money that established a foundation for future growth.

In terms of stability, AC's leaders sought to manage schools' relationships with their environments to protect them from interference and to support implementation. Although AC's focus at the time was chiefly on individual schools, its staff often appealed to districts on schools' behalf, either to exempt them from district requirements that interfered with the program or to mediate relations between schools and districts. In some cases, AC helped principals to write school improvement plans that placed AC at their center.[37]

The need for stability went further. Specifically, AC also depended on environments not to intrude on its turf. Though policy-supported standards and assessments had long been missing from US educational environments, the standards-based reform movement began to gather steam during precisely the period in the late 1990s when AC was seeking to scale up its network. States' success in developing standards and accountability assessments risked obviating the need for AC's own performance standards and reference exams. Instead, AC would have to deal with fifty different sets of state standards and assessments, all likely at different stages of development and coordination. Since the essential problem of instruction in AC was to bridge between standards and students' needs, this would certainly complicate matters across the board.

Thus, AC's success hinged on carefully reasoned and intentionally structured relationships among schools, its design, its own organization, and broader environments. For teachers to succeed in developing the knowledge, skills, and standards needed to enact instruction as intended, school-based design coaches and literacy coordinators would have to learn to be effective professional educators with only a few weeks of training, after which they would need to begin immediately supporting teachers' professional learning. This was work that few school leaders had historically done in the United States, and for which few school leaders had any academic or professional training. Failure to develop their capabilities would leave teachers without what developers saw as the most essential resource for supporting their professional learning. Indeed, to move AC to large-scale operations was to build an entire professional educational system, one level in each school, another level among schools, and a third in the central organization. In the late 1990s, AC's comparatively late launch found it operating at a much smaller scale than ASP and SFA. America's Choice would never reach the scale of SFA and ASP, owing both to the challenges of developing a professional education system and to turbulence in environmental support for comprehensive school reform.

Conclusion

In an environment that offered growing political pressure and fiscal support for results but weak and incoherent educational infrastructure, the states and the national government could offer little direct assistance to schools. This was the interveners' raison d'être.

So ASP, SFA, and AC faced a common problem: that of helping schools turn themselves from failing organizations into successful ones absent strong and coherent educational infrastructure. The interveners had to devise ways for practitioners to learn ambitious and unfamiliar practices while they unlearned the familiar practices that were widely used but that had defeated ambitious learning. The interveners would have to help teachers build bridges from their former practices to new ones, while teachers carried on in their existing roles and schools. In effect, the interveners were trying to fill a large gap that was created by the lack of an educational infrastructure that could support quality education for students and teachers.

ASP avoided detailed prescription of instruction because it feared mere mechanical implementation (which, as we will see in the next chapter, is precisely the problem with which SFA eventually struggled). Instead, ASP offered guidance for schools' culture, organization, and ideas, and sketched guidance for instruction in broad principles. But by offering such modest guidance to teachers in weak schools, ASP effectively delegated an enormous task to them: that of designing instructional programs and then either inventing or adapting the curriculum and practices to make them work. ASP believed that schools would find many sources of strength and resources in themselves and nearby organizations. But that posed two problems. To invent a new and ambitious instructional program would have been a daunting task for schools in privileged localities. How likely were weak teachers in underprivileged schools to get very far beyond the practices with which they were familiar, if they had to invent so much? And how likely were weak schools and organizations to have the strength to support such a radically different approach to education, when there were few precedents for it in educational practice? These would be central problems as ASP moved from design to practice.

SFA began with very detailed guidance for teaching that was intended to do two things that were in some tension: to supporting weak teachers in improving instruction from the beginning of their work with Success for All; and, within a year, supporting these same teachers in progressing to more adaptive and complex practices. A large problem was buried here. If the design placed great emphasis on very detailed guidance for early implementation by weak teachers, how likely were these same teachers to learn to quickly become more independent and expert? Could these teachers learn ambitious new practices while both unlearning their inherited practice and weaning themselves from detailed guidance, all while projecting the competence needed to secure the confidence of students, parents, and leaders? How could SFA develop the capability to support adaptive and flexible practice for more experienced teachers while developing the capability to support much more directive practice for beginning teachers? And how could the organization grow to meet the needs of more and more schools, while expanding the capability to offer them high-quality help at the same time? Where could it find the human and financial resources for this work? The harder SFA worked to solve problems in a rapidly growing base of schools, the more it had to compensate for weaknesses in environments. These would be central problems as SFA moved from design to practice.

Both ASP and SFA tried to help teachers learn their way into expert practice while unlearning the practices that impeded students' learning. AC also saw professional learning as central, and its design gave it a crucial role. America's Choice offered much more guidance for teaching than Accelerated Schools, but it was much less directive than Success for All. AC sought to marry the autonomy and flexibility it saw as hallmarks of expert teaching to the academic standards and examples of practice it saw as essential to such expertise. The glue in that marriage would be schools that supported teachers' learning with model classrooms, in-school coaches, and extended opportunities for professional learning. Yet how likely were teachers to learn an entirely new approach to their work while unlearning much of what they knew and while carrying on as competent professionals? And how likely were newly minted coaches to be able to teach teachers these new practices? These were the central problems as AC moved from design to practice.

One problem for all three interveners was whether the designs and schools offered suitable opportunities to learn new practices. A conventional way that intending professionals learn practice is in extended apprenticeships in which expert practitioners supervise them and in organizations that support and protect the work. Such learning is not easy, but the apprenticeship offers a combination of expert guidance, modeling, and opportunities to practice and revise in somewhat protected settings. Yet those things would not be available to teachers in schools that worked with the interveners, for the schools in which they worked were unusually weak and often troubled, and the "experts" who supervised them—the coaches and coordinators—typically were learning their new trade as they were trying to teach teachers. Could they quickly become effective teacher educators when none of them had ever used the curriculum or teaching practices that the designs required?

Efforts to answer that question affirmatively were complicated by working conditions. Teachers had to carry a full load of work in weak schools; they had to carry that load while trying to unlearn much of what they had known; they had to do so while learning much that was quite unfamiliar; and they had to work in rather unprotected settings that were not designed to support professional learning. Both the teachers and their coaches were apprentices in the sense that they had much to learn, but not in the sense that they had extended opportunities to learn new practices while working in protected settings with experts. That was an unavoidable consequence of taking schools as they were and improving them on the fly, but it impeded teachers' and coaches' efforts to build bridges from what they had done to what the interventions wanted them to do. It was a common problem as the interventions moved from design to practice.

In common usage design typically connotes a solution. For the interveners, design connoted a complex puzzle: specifically, in the relationships among the schools to be improved, the designs intended to improve them, their own organizations, and broader environments.

In this scheme, design included sketching the sorts of schools that ASP, SFA, and AC wanted to bring into existence; detailing practices within those schools; and developing the supporting practices, organizations, culture, and strategies for change. It included developing a multilayered "curriculum of improvement" to support the learning of students, teachers, leaders, and trainers, as all sought to learn to work differently in interaction with each other. It led to the development of the intervening organizations that would support this complex, interactive, multilevel learning enterprise. The designs were the interveners' innovative achievement, but their organizations were a signal invention, for they made it possible to create and operate national systems of schooling. But if the designs, professional education, and other support did not generate the intended changes in teaching, learning, management, and organization, then the problems of implementation that arose in schools would feed back on the interveners and their organizations. That also became a common problem as they moved from design to practice.

The challenges were enhanced by the interveners' position in US education. The schools that they wanted to change were part of the system of public education, yet the interveners had no authority or formal position in that system. Rather, they were independent nongovernment nonprofits with weak leverage on schools. Worse, they depended on the very agencies they were trying to change for evaluations that could establish their legitimacy, for money to fund large parts of their operations, and for Title I funds to support schools' purchase of their materials and services. They also needed the government to offer incentives for schools to adopt their designs. They were unusually deeply engaged with schools, yet that connection was tenuous, for schools could ignore them with little consequence. Given their aim to create deep and lasting change, that was inconvenient at best.

ASP, SFA, and AC had to build organizations that developed temporary, consensual relationships with schools in order to permanently transform them. They had to build organizations that could exert a potent influence on state schools while operating in the private sector. Their organizations had to enable individual schools to become effective alternatives to existing elementary education, to turn their networks into effective alternative systems of schooling, and to do these things despite working in larger, often ineffective school districts in generally unhelpful educational environments. None of these things had been done before, and no one knew much about how to do them.

THREE

The Implementation Puzzle

By the turn of the millennium in 2000, SFA, AC, and ASP had achieved unusual success. All three had rolled out large-scale operations, and an emerging body of research was providing evidence of effectiveness. For example, an external evaluation of Accelerated Schools found that enactment of key elements of the program yielded gains in student achievement by the fifth year.[1] An external, first-year evaluation of America's Choice found that coaches and school leaders were enacting key features of the design intended to develop teachers' knowledge of the New Standards Performance Standards, of the New Standards Reference Exams, and Readers and Writers Workshops.[2] In 2001, SFA cofounders Robert Slavin and Nancy Madden asserted that Success for All was "arguably the most extensively evaluated school reform model ever to exist," and that "the results of evaluations of dozens of Success for All schools in all parts of the United States and five other countries clearly show that the program increases student reading performance."[3] And an independent meta-analysis categorized Success for All as showing "strongest evidence of effectiveness" and America's Choice and Accelerated Schools as showing "promising evidence of effectiveness."[4]

This combination of scale and effectiveness was a formidable accomplishment: it was the first time in US history that student achievement in weak schools and unsupportive environments had been improved on such a large scale. Even so, the successes were a good deal less than what the interveners had expected. Despite fundamental differences in their core strategies and in the details of their experience, they all faced a common problem: many schools were more successful in developing capability for limited use of program resources than in developing capability for consistent, high-level use of program resources. Schools in all three networks did succeed in establishing new organizational structures, new leadership roles, and (in Success for All and America's Choice) new but limited instructional routines. However, all three interveners found it very difficult to realize their core ambitions for instructional practice in large numbers of schools: "early intervention and relentlessness" in the case of Success for All, "professional instructional practice" in the case of America's Choice, and "powerful learning" in the case of Accelerated Schools.

Commonly, this mix of success and struggle would be described in terms of "weak implementation": that is, as externally developed "solutions" not being "executed" as intended by schools. But, in the case of our three interveners, the implementation puzzle was much more complicated. Indeed, if the design puzzle was to structure conditions among schools, designs, organizations, and environments in order to increase the potential for effectiveness, then the implementation puzzle was to manage interactions within and among these four domains over time in order to realize that potential.

All three interveners struggled to do so. Amid a rapid increase in scale, schools and environments interacted to establish initial conditions that challenged (rather than supported) the development of teachers' capabilities. Strengths and weaknesses in still-evolving designs interacted with schools and environments to increase potential for low-level use of program resources while reducing the potential for high-level use of program resources. Finally, interveners' still-emerging organizations exacerbated, rather than ameliorated, variable support for low-level versus high-level use. The result was a sort of within-network incoherence in which dysfunctional interactions among schools, designs, intervening organizations, and environments undermined, rather than supported, the development of teachers' capabilities.

The preceding dynamics were exacerbated by four additional problems experienced by all three interveners. One problem was that all three began by taking schools as they were, rather than starting anew with charter schools. Taking schools as they found them meant that they would have to dramatically change teaching and school leadership while school personnel continued to carry on full-time work in difficult schools. No one had time off to learn new practices and knowledge, to practice their use, and to unlearn much of what they knew and did. Nor could they do that work in protected environments with expert practitioners. Some learning could be done on the fly, as teachers read about the interventions or observed each other, if they could make sense of what they saw and heard. But a great deal of it required that teachers and leaders be taught. The trainers in each program were, above all else, teacher educators and leader educators. But this professional education would have to fit in around regular daily work. It was not like teaching novice nurses and doctors in hospitals, but more like reeducating doctors and nurses who had plenty of experience as unsuccessful practitioners, as they continued to work in settings in which they had done poorly.

A second problem was that developing new capabilities for practice was something that had to happen simultaneously and in coordinated ways across multiple practitioners, in schools and beyond. Teachers would have to work together on curriculum and pedagogy; school leaders would have to work closely with teachers; and teachers and school leaders would have to work closely with intervention field staff. All would have to see and understand relationships that they had not known before and coordinate things that they had never coordinated, including instructional work, language, and artifacts. Such coordination was very unfamiliar in most US schools. Achieving it would require new organizational structures, new sorts of leadership, new approaches to teaching and learning, new school cultures, and new relationships with field staff. Moreover, each of these elements fit into each of the designs in very particular ways, so that effective implementation required that they be put into practice in proper relation to all of the other elements. If the individual elements of the designs were very demanding for weak schools, coordination among them added greatly to the demand.

A third problem was that all three interveners sought to do these things in environments that offered little support and many obstacles. Indeed, at the same time that they provided financial support and aided recruiting, agencies in the environment often worked directly against the efforts of the interveners. It was not unusual for district central offices to urge schools that had adopted one of the three interventions to adopt one or more other improvement programs, even though that had potential to weaken implementation. Nor was it unusual for state or local school systems that had supported schools' adoption of an intervention to change the means or the schedule for evaluation. And it was not unusual for the superintendent who had shepherded the adoption of one or more interventions to quickly be succeeded by another who had different interests, concerns, and strategies. In addition, the environment lacked essential educational infrastructure that would have helped the schools and interveners: for example, coordinated curricula, examinations, and professional education that supported a coherent approach to teaching and learning. Instead, state and local policies often diverged or even conflicted, as did tests and curricula. Finally, teacher education in colleges and universities did not prepare many teachers to do good work in high-poverty schools.

A fourth problem arose from the three interveners' laudable ambition and responsibility. All three had set noble but very difficult ambitions for themselves: specifically, developing the capability to provide ambitious instruction and greatly improved learning in America's weakest schools. Where many earlier developers had taken little responsibility for effective use of their programs, ASP, AC, and SFA were so committed to improving education that they took extensive responsibility for helping schools to use the designs well. They designed their organizations to do that, they arranged for field staff to support schools' work, they raised money for these and other related efforts, and more. This support for implementation was the interveners' comparative advantage, and it helps to explain their success. But because there was such a great distance between the interveners' ambitions (on the one hand) and schools' capabilities and environmental support (on the other), change was quite difficult, and many problems developed as schools used the intervention designs. Such problems always have been felt somewhere, and for most previous reforms they were felt chiefly in the programs' failures in practice. But in this case, because the interveners took responsibility for implementation, the schools' problems became the interveners' problems. Their efforts to do a better job and act more responsibly added greatly to the already extraordinary demands on their staffs and organizations. Their comparative advantage also was a comparative disadvantage.

The breadth, complexity, and span of the interveners' work precludes an exhaustive account of their experiences engaging the implementation puzzle. Instead, in the remainder of the chapter, we provide a snapshot of the ways in which they experienced the implementation puzzle by summarizing key patterns of dysfunctional interactions among designs, schools, organizations, and environments that resulted in incoherence and weak capabilities. As we do so, we also highlight key instances when one or more of these four common problems exacerbated those interactions.

With that, the chapter brings us to the point at which the interveners stood in the early 2000s. They had succeeded in establishing large-scale networks that showed remarkable success in changing practice and student achievement, yet they exhibited many of the enduring and stubborn problems that they had originally set out to tackle. Those problems were far from the interveners' creation alone, but they were theirs alone to solve.

Success for All

Cast in terms of its core strategy, SFA succeeded through the early 2000s in supporting teachers in novice, low-level enactment of its instructional design, though it struggled in supporting teachers in expert, high-level enactment. Through a period of rapid scale-up in the mid- to late 1990s, teachers were succeeding in using the program's detailed curriculum materials to effect a quick change in instructional practice, thus establishing a new, higher, and more coordinated base level of operations. However, teachers struggled to build on this success to begin identifying and addressing the specific needs of individual students. With that, they also struggled to initiate an upward spiral of enthusiasm, commitment, and (especially) instructional improvement.

Consequently, as SFA moved into its second decade of operations, an estimated 75% of teachers were locked into a pattern of novice, mechanistic implementation of low-level routines, with only 25% of teachers progressing to the goal of identifying and addressing the academic and nonacademic needs of students.[5] The result was what SFA staffers described as a "plateau effect" on student achievement well below the program goal of on-grade-level reading performance.

Any number of strategic decisions might have reduced the risks of such problems emerging: for example, working in newly established charter schools that did not have a legacy of failure; advancing a less comprehensive and less training-intensive design; working in schools adjacent to excellent schools of education; and/or abdicating responsibility for success and, with that, the need to adapt the design and organization in response to schools and environments. But, again, SFA took schools as they were, advanced a comprehensive and ambitious design, worked in any and all environments, and took responsibility for success.

Interactions: Schools and Environments

The problems began with dysfunctional interactions between schools and environments. These interactions resulted in SFA recruiting large numbers of schools with weak initial capabilities, weak commitment to improvement, and weak commitment to SFA. They also resulted in teachers whose capabilities and predispositions provided a weak foundation for pursuing Success for All's goal of relentless, adaptive, locally responsive use.

As reported by long-serving members, initial efforts to scale up Success for All in the early 1990s were successful in drawing schools that they described as "classic early adopters." Motivated by the gathering standards-and-accountability movement, these were schools already committed to improvement, often with newly appointed and unusually able leaders, and often given new freedom by districts to pursue school-wide improvement. These same schools enacted SFA's program adoption process with integrity, including the requirement of an 80% vote for program adoption by all instructional staff. The result was an initial, installed base of schools that, even though struggling, were committed to SFA as program for deep, long-term, school-wide improvement.

However, environments soon proved to be both a blessing and a curse. Over the 1990s, increasing policy pressure to improve student achievement interacted with increasing support for comprehensive school reform both to (a) drive up the installed base of Success for All schools and (b) drive down the initial commitment and capabilities of newly adopting schools. Over this period, Goals 2000 and the Improving America's Schools Act of 1994 provided resources and incentives for establishing state-level systems of standards and assessments with which to hold schools accountable for improving student achievement. At the same time, federal policies such as Title I of IASA, the Comprehensive School Reform Demonstration Act of 1997, and the Reading Excellence Act of 1998 provided billions of dollars to newly pressured schools to adopt comprehensive school reform programs.

One result was great interest in Success for All, either because schools identified it as a promising program or because schools were pushed by districts, states, and even courts to adopt "research-validated" programs. From 1997/98 to 1999/2000, Success for All doubled its installed base, from roughly 750 schools to roughly 1,500 schools. Another result was that the large number of new schools overwhelmed the possibility of SFA ensuring that the program adoption process was enacted with integrity. Indeed, both SFA staff members and external researchers reported that the process was widely compromised.[6] Yet another result was a regression from classic early adopter to modal, impacted, Title I school. As recalled by SFA cofounder and president Nancy Madden in a 2003 interview,

We really began to work with a very, very weak group of schools, a very, very impacted group of schools. And those schools tended to have a number of characteristics. They have 100 percent poverty. They have all kinds of students moving all the time, as well as teachers moving all the time, just a great deal of just teacher mobility. They also have principals moving a lot. They also have superintendents moving a lot. So you've got all kinds of things tearing apart the organizations at the school level, and that it makes it harder for them to do anything systematically and at-depth.[7]

Especially challenging were the capabilities and predispositions of teachers in newly recruited schools, both of which had roots in teachers' interactions with US educational environments. One problem was teachers' professional preparation. Some teachers simply did not have any. Over the 1990s and into the early 2000s, lax certification requirements made it entirely possible for schools pressed to fill teaching positions to hire uncertified teachers, if only on a temporary basis. Yet to say that a teacher was certified was often not to say much, as undergraduate teacher education at the time often did little to prepare teachers to teach reading to large populations of at-risk students. Explained one experienced SFA trainer in a 2003 interview:

We were being presumptuous thinking that teachers were coming into this knowing how to teach reading . . . a lot of teachers did and a lot of teachers didn't, particularly in the schools that we work in. They're usually the lowest performing schools in their districts. They're trying to get staff and keep staff. And there's so many times that the universities . . . don't have strong reading programs. Sometimes it's just because people haven't taken any of those classes, because they're not certified and they were just stuck in the classroom. And we were making assumptions that these teachers had knowledge of teaching reading.[8]

Another problem was teachers' predispositions toward externally supported school improvement.[9] On the one hand, many teachers had long experience in districts prone to heavy-handed, external intervention that was at odds with strong traditions of local control and professional autonomy. In this case, the result was a predisposition to see external support as bureaucratic, unwarranted, and unwelcome: that is, as a sort of coercive intervention that evoked either resistance or defiant compliance. On the other hand, many teachers were also experiencing new policy pressure to improve student achievement. In this case, the result was a predisposition to see external support as technocratic, warranted, and welcome: that is, as a sort of enabling resource that, if used exactly as described by developers, would function as a quick fix. Neither of these dispositions was consistent with aspirations for SFA to serve as a resource supporting expert, locally adaptive use.

Interactions: Schools, Environments, and Design

Again, SFA was committed to taking schools as they were and to begin working toward program goals for practice and achievement. However, as an apparently favorable policy environment drove rapid scale-up, one concern for SFA became supporting teachers' success in enacting new instructional practices. Another concern became preventing their backslide into past (and ineffective) practices. Robert Slavin, SFA cofounder and chairman, explained in a 2003 interview,

> You don't want a situation in which every teacher doesn't know what the program is supposed to look like, makes up whatever they're going to do, and basically slides back into their usual practices. That's been the history of education reform since the earth cooled: wonderful ideas that worked in the first few schools, and when you try to go to your fifth or sixth school, much less your tenth or twelfth school, it's gone. There's no trace. It's not happening. That has been the history. The forms may remain, but the function is gone. The flag may be on the front of the school, but there's nothing inside that you can pick out. Even before Success for All, we did cooperative learning. Before that, I studied mastery learning and other things. Over and over and over again, you see the progression from a few excited people saying, "It's going to solve all my problems!" and, then, no trace among schools that think that they're implementing something.[10]

Over the 1990s, the Success for All design evolved in interaction with schools and environments, with the intent of both supporting success and preventing problems. This evolution was driven by experience in schools, new research, and new commercial materials that were incorporated into the program. Yet, ironically, the result was to increase the potential for rote, mechanistic use of program resources while doing little to increase the potential for expert, adaptive use.

Taking schools as they were, and recognizing weaknesses in the commitment and capabilities of newly recruited teachers, SFA developers placed a strong emphasis on providing very detailed guidance for the teachers' role in direct instruction, complemented by a detailed scope and sequence of reading strategies, detailed units and lessons, and detailed daily pacing guides. In some cases, the guidance went so far as to script teachers' presentation of letter sounds and reading comprehension strategies. Given the weaknesses of many teachers, and given the risk of backsliding into past practice, SFA developers saw such detailed guidance as warranted.

At the same time, during this period of rapid scale-up, adaptation took a backseat to consistency as a first-order concern. Indeed, SFA developers did little to develop routines, information resources, and guidance to support expert, adaptive use. While the Success for All reading program provided some flexibility in unit planning (especially for reading comprehension in grades 2–6), and while the program placed a premium on teachers' in-the-moment diagnosis and remediation in the context of students' cooperative learning tasks, it provided few resources to support teachers in leveraging these opportunities to adapt instruction to address the needs and problems of students. Further, knowledge of how to leverage opportunities for diagnosis and adaptation was still emerging both in broader environments and among SFA developers and trainers, and it had yet to be formalized in program materials. Still further, it would have been very difficult and expensive to formalize adaptive use in material resources at the required level of detail, whether in lesson-by-lesson guidance for routine problem solving or by setting out the knowledge base needed to manage nonroutine problems.

Weak capabilities and predispositions in newly recruited teachers interacted with strengths and weaknesses in the Success for All reading program to put pressure on school leaders. As the installed base of Success for All schools grew, and as SFA's trainers were stretched across more and more schools, school leaders became increasingly responsible for developing teachers' capabilities. Given strong support for low-level, consistent use, school leaders needed to manage teachers' understandings of the program not as bureaucratic or technocratic but, instead, as a resource that ultimately aimed to support teachers' agency and adaptation. Given weak support for high-level, adaptive use, school leaders needed to transcend the limits of the reading program to help teachers achieve those goals. Given that SFA was taking schools as they were, leaders had to do all of this in the context of teachers' day-to-day work, in schools that had long struggled to improve instructional practice and outcomes.

Yet Success for All's leadership component had evolved to mirror its instructional component. Success for All provided extensive guidance for consistent, low-level leadership practice: for example, instituting the ninety-minute reading block, assessing students quarterly, and observing instruction to assess fidelity of implementation. At the same time, Success for All provided comparatively weak guidance for adaptive, high-level leadership practice: for example, analyzing quarterly assessment results to identify instances and patterns of success and struggle, strategically grouping students into classrooms to increase the potential for instructional effectiveness, and collaborating with teachers to diagnose and address problems of instruction. And, again, variable support for low-level versus high-level leadership centered on the same issues as variable support for instruction: consistency (rather than adaptation) as the most pressing concern amid rapid growth; emergent understanding of expert instructional leadership practice having yet to be formalized in material resources; and the difficulty and costs of formalizing such knowledge at a detailed level.

Interactions: Schools, Environments, Design, and Organizations

Thus schools, environments, and design interacted to place tremendous demands on SFA as an organization: specifically, on its training organization. All were interacting to increase potential for low-level, mechanistic enactment of the instructional design while doing little to increase potential for high-level, adaptive enactment. With that, it fell on SFA's training organization both to establish consistent enactment across schools and then to support the progression to more adaptive enactment. Indeed, the linkages between first trainers and leaders and then leaders and teachers were among the most fundamental points of coordination in the Success for All design.

Yet, over the 1990s, the training organization itself had evolved to exacerbate rather than resolve variable potential for low-level versus high-level enactment. The problems began with rapid expansion in the training organization. Growing in proportion to its network of schools, the training organization doubled in size for three consecutive years, peaking at 250 trainers in 2001. Thus, in each of those years, 50% of trainers were new, and another 25% had only one year's experience. Moreover, in recruiting these trainers, SFA failed to identify a labor pool of expert trainers on which to draw. As such, SFA recruited trainers from Success for All schools. While these trainers were committed to Success for All, few had knowledge of how to enact each of the program components at a high level, and fewer yet had knowledge of how to help weak and uncommitted schools to do so. Indeed, in a 2003 interview, one experienced SFA manager explained that many of the newly recruited trainers had the very same weaknesses as the schools that they were to support.

When we grew so big, in 1999, we had some trainers who were well-versed in understanding diagnostic instruction, and we had many who were not. We had many trainers who not only did not understand diagnostic instruction but who had a hard time understanding the basic philosophical principles that support diagnostic instruction.[11]

The problems continued with SFA's dependence on the training organization for revenues. Despite their weaknesses, the self-funding, fee-for-service nature of SFA's training organization required that trainers enter the field immediately, both to cover the costs of their initial training and equipment and to generate operating revenues for SFA as an organization. Had it succeeded in identifying external sources of funding to support the development of the training organization, SFA might have been able to keep newly recruited trainers "off-line" for a period of time to develop their knowledge and capabilities. But, again, SFA found no donors willing to directly fund capacity building within SFA. SFA's novice trainers entered the field immediately.

The problems stretched further, into difficulties developing systems to support the work and professional development of trainers. These differences directly parallel those experienced in supporting Success for All teachers and leaders. Concerned with ensuring success and preventing problems, SFA developed resources that provided strong support for low-level, consistent training: for example, training scripts focused on supporting low-level, consistent implementation in schools, and observation protocols that focused on evaluating consistency of implementation in schools. Yet formal support for expert, locally responsive training practice was much weaker: for example, protocols supporting dialogue between trainers and leaders around substantive issues of instruction and achievement, or opportunities for trainers to learn how to mentor schools in expert use of the program. Instead, staff members reported that expert knowledge of training practice emerged first among small groups of experienced and geographically proximal trainers, and that this knowledge spread only as new trainers were incorporated into these "communities of training practice." However, these communities of training practice were also stretched thin by the rapid growth of the training organization. As explained in a 2003 interview by Barbara Haxby, SFA's director of implementation,

How do you target change? How do you make thoughtful adaptations in the program? How do you help schools be able to target and troubleshoot? A lot of that was happening very informally within our organization, because we were a very small staff. If there's only six of us sitting around a table, then you say, "What do you do with . . . Well, what if . . . ". It was all at that much more "sitting around a table" kind of level. When we added 70 trainers per year, we got systems for training. But what really lagged behind was the whole system for how do we monitor and how do we address implementation and issues of implementation. You can't just be about, "Is the program in place?" You've got to be looking at the outcomes. You've got to be able to shift what people are doing. You have to be able to talk to people about what their goals are.[12]

Result: Weaknesses in Coherence and Capabilities

In embracing the design puzzle, SFA had gone to great lengths to structure positive relationships among schools, environments, its design, and its own organization. Moreover, a combination of research and experience suggested great potential for effective, large-scale operations.

At the same time, the implementation puzzle—that is, the challenge of managing dynamic interactions in these four domains—resulted in a sort of within-program incoherence. On the one hand, the first principles of Success for All included intervening early and relentlessly, at the first sign of problems, by adapting, coordinating, and evaluating academic and nonacademic services for students. On the other hand, SFA provided weak support for such work. Instead, from its inception through the late 1990s, dysfunctional interactions among the schools and environments drove the evolution of the design and the organization in ways that provided strong support for low-level, consistent use while providing comparatively weak support for high-level, adaptive use.

This incoherence, in turn, resulted in weak capabilities among teachers. Many teachers interpreted Success for All as either bureaucratic or technocratic and not professional. Further, whether out of defiance or enthusiasm, many teachers enacted Success for All mechanically (and not adaptively and responsively). In a 2003 interview, Barbara Haxby recalled a school visit in which she watched a teacher interpret and enact Success for All through a technocratic lens. In the context of a reading comprehension lesson, the teacher tightly followed a set of questions scripted in the curriculum, and she solicited students' responses in whole-group discussion. However, the teacher appeared unaware that students' responses were actually incorrect, she did nothing to discern why students' responses were incorrect, and she did nothing to help the students work with the text to amend their responses. Haxby saw the root of the problem as lying in the teacher's view of instruction as a matter of her performance, and not as a complex puzzle that involves actively managing relationships among her performance, academic content, and students' learning. Explained Haxby:

There's still a perception from this teacher that her job is to deliver instruction. Her job is what she does, standing up there in front of the classroom. And if she does all the right things, she's OK. She doesn't perceive her job as saying, "My job is to understand where every single child is in this classroom in terms of their reading skills." Somehow she still is thinking, "Where I need to be is following a particular instructional plan." The focus is on her own performance. And she views her performance by what she does. Not what the kids do or what the transfer is between what she does and what the kids do.[13]

And, again, the most formidable problem faced by SFA was that, given dysfunctional interactions among its schools and the environments in which they operated, both its design and its organization had actually evolved to drive teachers in exactly that direction.

America's Choice

Cast in terms of its core strategy, AC struggled in the early 2000s to create a professional education system successful in developing teachers' capabilities to plan and enact instruction that was responsive both to high standards for student achievement and the immediate needs of students. As in Success for All, teachers succeeded in low-level use of the America's Choice instructional frameworks, which guided time allocation, student grouping, classroom layout, and instructional tasks. However, teachers struggled to analyze the performance and needs of students, select texts appropriate for groups of students performing at particular levels, construct instructional tasks that used these texts to develop students' mastery of particular academic standards, and then engage in in-the-moment diagnosis and response as they enacted these instructional tasks with groups of students.

An external evaluation of America's Choice showed ratios comparable to Success for All.[14] Some 65% of teachers succeeded in low-level use of the instructional frameworks. Yet, with respect to high-level use, only 40% incorporated standards in designing and analyzing instruction, and only 24% used analysis of student work to drive the design and enactment of instruction. Anecdotally, AC staff members reported that these problems were more acute in reading than in writing.

Like SFA, AC could have taken measures to reduce the risk of such problems: for example, working only in schools that agreed to replace the principal and/or reconstitute the staff; reducing standards for performance and the knowledge demands of the design; working only with districts that consented to give AC complete control of schools; and/or highlighting successes while masking problems. But, like SFA, AC took schools as they were, advanced a comprehensive and ambitious design, worked in any and all environments, and took responsibility for success.

Interactions: Schools and Environments

As with SFA, the problems began with dysfunctional interactions among schools and environments. Indeed, AC was predicated on interdependent weaknesses in the schools and their environments, and it was little surprise that AC encountered these weaknesses as it scaled up its network of schools. Like SFA, AC leaders and staffers reported recruiting large numbers of unstable schools weakly prepared to pursue its ambitions for instruction. More so than SFA, AC leaders and staffers reported that these schools existed in school districts that both effected problems in schools and functioned as barriers to enacting America's Choice.

While SFA reported an "early adopter" phenomenon among its initial base of schools, AC did not. Rather, AC staff members reported that even its first group of forty-five schools were afflicted by the usual problems of underperforming schools, many with roots in broader educational environments: for example, weaknesses in teachers' and leaders' capabilities; annual student mobility rates that sometimes exceeded 50%; high turnover of teachers and leaders; and community poverty.

Again, AC staff members reported that problems in schools interacted with problems in districts, with some of the interactions resulting from activity in broader educational environments. Recalling experiences with large-scale education reform prior to establishing AC, Marc Tucker, AC's founder, captured the view of many in the organization in observing that "our long-standing conviction that districts matter was confirmed."[15]

For example, many of the problems in schools actually had deep roots in district policies and procedures, such as district assignment practices that had the weakest teachers accumulating in the weakest schools (such as those using America's Choice), contractual restrictions that limited the opportunity for school leaders to work with teachers, and constraints on the use of time for teacher meetings and work groups. Further, the usual (and voluminous) mix of ever-churning, district-level programs drew attention away from America's Choice and sent mixed signals to schools about its importance. Still further, the same policy pressures and resources that were drawing schools into comprehensive school reform were also drawing in districts, which further fragmented district-level priorities and operations. As explained by one member of AC's training organization:

At the district level, there are schools doing Modern Red Schoolhouse or SFA or America's Choice, and there are districts within districts. And at our school, which is supposed to be AC, there are so many other initiatives. We have a new $100,000 arts program that is supposed to permeate all classrooms. It can get pretty confusing.[16]

However, even though districts mattered, AC had little (if any) leverage to refashion the priorities, operations, or capabilities of districts to support school-level implementation of America's Choice. Policy and philanthropic initiatives that supported the growth of America's Choice (e.g., New American Schools and the Obey-Porter Comprehensive School Reform Demonstration Act of 1997) channeled funding directly to schools to support school-level decisions to adopt particular comprehensive school reform programs. As such, AC worked mainly (and directly) with individual schools, with neither the access nor the means to influence district decision making. Yet district decisions often impeded implementation. For example, AC executive Judy Codding described one large, urban district that fielded a district-wide professional development program that not only did little to support the implementation of America's Choice but, in fact, directly conflicted with key elements of the instructional design. As Codding explained, "they're spending millions on America's Choice and might actually be hindering implementation."[17]

Interactions: Schools, Environments, and Design

As in SFA, policy-driven growth of the AC network increased the risk that newly recruited teachers would not be able to apprehend and enact the America's Choice instructional design as intended by its developers. Taking schools as they were, success depended on teachers unlearning and shedding many deeply entrenched understandings and practices. Success also depended on teachers developing new understandings and capabilities for defining goals, enacting their role in instruction, assessing student performance, and collaborating with colleagues and school leaders. And, again, success depended on doing all of the preceding in the context of teachers' ongoing, day-to-day work.

The steepest demands lay in developing understandings of and capabilities to enact instruction that was simultaneously responsive to students and to standards. For example, Dorothy Fowler, AC's director of literacy, explained that successfully enacting guided reading (a key component of Readers Workshop, the America's Choice design for reading instruction) placed new knowledge demands on teachers who were well-practiced in the rote use of conventional basal reading programs.

She also explained that it took a fine eye to detect the difference between reading instruction as intended by America's Choice and conventional reading instruction.

If you just walked into a classroom [with traditional reading groups] and our classroom . . . you could go "oh, these are the same." But they're not the same. The demands on the teacher in a basal program [are less] because the text is chosen for you. The teacher doesn't need to think about what's the right book for this child. The text is there. In the basal program you don't need to think about what's the question that I should ask this child that will really get them to use this strategy effectively for comprehension or decoding. The text gives you the questions that you're going to ask and the focus for the lesson. And the notion is that if we just do all of those focuses by the end of the year they will have been exposed enough times that it will belong to them.

Whereas what America's Choice asks is for the teacher . . . to decide on a focus ahead of time because you saw in children's reading performances or in their conversations something that shows you that there was a need. We're going to make you choose the book for those children. And it's not just page 76 of your basal. We're going to ask you then to choose the specific question or the specific set up, scenario, modeling, think aloud, whatever . . . and to then make this clear to that guided reading group. And then we're going to ask you to assess it not based on a pull out from your reproducible assessment notebook but based on observation, based on running records, based on on-site assessments.[18]

As in Success for All, America's Choice sought both to support teachers in successfully enacting its instructional designs while preventing teachers from misunderstanding and co-opting them. However, even during its first year of operations, schools and environments interacted with AC's still-emerging design to increase the potential for low-level use while reducing the potential for high-level use.

As with Success for All, the problems began with variable formalization or elaboration of low-level versus high-level use. The America's Choice instructional frameworks were elaborated at a sufficient level of detail that they could be used by many teachers at a base level with existing knowledge and capabilities. Teachers succeeded in grouping students, arranging the classroom, and developing, sequencing, and pacing common instructional tasks.

At the same time, America's Choice provided little formal guidance for how to use student assessments and standards to do such work strategically, in ways that increased the potential for all students to perform at high standards. As with Success for All, formalizing guidance for high-level use would have been expensive and difficult. Moreover, in the case of America's Choice, doing so was also at odds with an ethos of professionalism and with the belief that teachers (not material resources) were the locus of expert instructional knowledge. However, weaknesses in the initial capabilities of newly recruited teachers (themselves a consequence of broader weaknesses in professional education and knowledge) left many feeling lost without explicit directions for what, when, and how to teach. Explained Dorothy Fowler, "what they'd really like is that we tell them what books to have, when to put [students] in those books, when to change those books. And the reason our teachers think like this is because that's what we (in the field of education) have done [to them]. We've always given them tools that didn't ask them to apply what they know. What America's Choice is asking for is a very different kind of teaching."[19] In a 2005 interview, reflecting on early experiences, Marc Tucker, AC's founder, concurred:

(Teachers) wanted more and more and more instructions. They wanted more and more content. They wanted to be told what to do. Should that have surprised us? No. Did it disappoint us? Yes. . . . It's just what we've learned. That's the kind of stuff you learn about by field testing stuff, and delivering services. You don't do it sitting in your office. And when we did it, that's what we found. They need a whole lot more scaffolding.[20]

Indeed, variable elaboration of low-level versus high-level use increased the demands on the America's Choice design for teachers' school-based professional learning. Collaboration among teachers and school leaders was intended to create opportunities to convey knowledge of high-level use through methods of discourse, modeling, and practice-and-critique.

But there were problems here, as well. One problem was with the model classroom design. The model classroom was to be the key to teachers' learning: the context in which teachers and school leaders would work through implementation, experiment, learn from experience, and create a working example from which others could learn. However, with just one model classroom, school-wide rollout of America's Choice progressed very slowly, with some teachers not having direct contact with the America's Choice instructional frameworks until many months after schools had begun implementation, and with novice teachers continuing to work amid persistent dysfunction within the school. The effect was to impede the development of coordinated instructional practice among teachers as well as the development of school-wide norms supporting implementation. It also opened up opportunity for realities and dysfunction in schools, districts, and broader environments to undermine America's Choice before it could find its legs in schools, thus eroding confidence in the program. For example, reflecting on early implementation, Larry Molinaro, AC's director of research, explained that the slow rollout of America's Choice ran up against the growing reality of standards-based reform:

For a long time you would start at the second grade and then you would have this slow roll-out. In some districts people were frustrated that we weren't getting to all of the grade levels fast enough. So, then what happens is if you don't get to the third grade classroom until April and they're testing in March?[21]

Another problem was with the design for school leadership. The America's Choice design already placed extensive knowledge demands on school leaders, and problems in the variable elaboration of instructional practice and in the model classroom increased those demands. However, many school leaders were themselves novices, both in instructional leadership (in general) and in America's Choice, in particular. In a 2002 interview, Peter Hill, who preceded Larry Molinaro as AC's director of research, explained that the risk in AC's initial schools was that school leaders would be weak in knowledge and credibility, and perhaps even "just one page ahead of their colleagues."[22] Further, as in Success for All, support for school leaders in America's Choice was weaker than the support for teachers, and for many of the same reasons: weak knowledge of instructional leadership in education writ large; weak knowledge of instructional leadership among program developers (especially as compared to knowledge of instructional practice); knowledge of instructional leadership emerging in tacit form among more experienced schools and trainers, but only as they enacted the program; and challenges sharing this tacit knowledge among a rapidly growing network of schools.

Problems with the leadership design would stay with America's Choice well into the 2000s. In a 2005 interview, Larry Molinaro explained that "we fundamentally are handing off [to coaches] the project management for implementation in the schools right at the beginning. And, I don't know that we prepare them."[23] Drawing on earlier experiences, he explained further:

We didn't actually come in with training around when you're a coach, how do you facilitate a conversation? What are good questions that you ask, or how do you ask good questions? How do you give feedback? How do you see feedback? How do you help with what we call objections? So, there was a lot around our expectations of the coaches in the schools that we weren't very good at really stating clearly or with a fair level of specificity. And then, we didn't even support (their practice).[24]

Interactions: Schools, Environments, Design, and Organizations

Schools, environments, and the design interacted to place heavy demands on AC's central organization. These included the need to provide operational support for scoring reference exams and reporting results. While such work was absolutely central, it was a responsibility with which AC occasionally struggled.

More importantly, these demands included the need for AC trainers to support implementation. As with SFA, relationships between field staff and school leaders and then between school leaders and teachers represented fundamental points of coordination with the program. With that, AC's training organization assumed primary responsibility for transcending all of the preceding to realize AC's ambitions for instruction and student achievement. As the AC network grew, the training organization would have to support more teachers and school leaders with more diverse backgrounds, all at work in schools of varying (and often weak) capabilities, in unsupportive environments, with few formal resources, and with shortcomings in the design for teachers' school-based professional learning.

Yet AC also experienced a series of cascading problems that resulted in its training organization doing more to increase potential for low-level use than to increase potential for high-level use, and for many of the same reasons as SFA. AC struggled to recruit experienced and expert trainers. Instead, it recruited trainers who were new to both external coaching and to AC. That, in turn, created an urgent need to devise opportunities and resources to support the professional development of newly recruited novice trainers. AC did so in two ways. First, newly recruited trainers participated in the same initial professional development opportunities as school leaders. While this was enough to create base-level understandings of AC, it meant that trainers knew scarcely more than those they were to teach. Second, the small size of AC's central organization enabled AC to continue developing trainers' capabilities much as in SFA: not through formally developed and highly refined professional development systems but, instead, in small, informal communities of training practice.

All this was exacerbated by travel demands. As the AC network grew in size and area, AC trainers simply had to cover more turf. One consequence was fatigue. One New York-based trainer supported schools that ranged from Long Island to Salmon River, New York, which was closer to Montreal than to her Manhattan home.[25] Reflecting on the stress of such work, she remarked half in jest, "You wake up in a hotel, and you don't know what state you're in." Another consequence was strain on the informal communities of practice that supported trainers' learning. Yet another consequence was cost. Looking back on this period, Marc Tucker, AC's founder, wrote that "travel costs were dominating our budget, and the growing travel burden was destroying our staff."[26]

The combined effect of these interacting problems was a training organization capable of providing low-level training support for low-level enactment of instruction in many schools, yet lacking capabilities to provide high-level training support for the high-level enactment of instruction in many schools. Even the most talented staffers had difficulty developing common understandings of AC's instructional designs and their implementation. For example, trainers agreed that a main professional development activity would be the analysis of students' work, yet they consistently differed about what work was "on-standard," what was not, and why. If AC's staff could not agree on what was on-standard, there was little chance that consensus could be reached in schools. Likewise, as field staff worked with school leaders, they were beset with questions about what counted as adequate implementation and to what extent schools could adapt the model to their needs. And, again, they struggled to provide consistent responses across schools.

Result: Weaknesses in Coherence and Capabilities

As with SFA, AC's efforts to manage the design puzzle yielded evidence of success effecting improvement in instruction and student achievement in a large network of schools. Yet, at the same time, the implementation puzzle again resulted in a sort of within-program incoherence in which dysfunctional interactions among schools, environments, the design, and the central organization undermined the development of teachers' capabilities to heed both students and standards in designing and enacting instruction. Schools and environments interacted to create initial conditions that would challenge high-level use of the model. While the America's Choice design placed considerable cognitive and organizational burdens on these teachers and school leaders, it provided much stronger support for low-level use as compared to high-level use. Likewise, rapid growth in AC's training organization had it also providing much stronger support for low-level versus high-level use. The result, predictably, was that many schools succeeded in low-level enactment of AC, while many struggled to progress to high-level enactment.

Just as SFA underestimated the challenge of supporting high-level instructional practice using materials as a primary resource, AC underestimated the challenge of supporting high-level instructional practice by developing its own system of professional education. And, as in SFA, these resulting difficulties caused frustration and bewilderment in the AC organization, where many could not understand why the training and support that they offered schools did not more consistently translate into improved performance. As explained by one top staffer, "things fall apart at the school."[27] Yet, in both cases, the most formidable piece of the puzzle at hand was that, for both SFA and AC, their designs and organizations were as much problem as solution.

Accelerated Schools

ASP also experienced the signature problem of more schools succeeding in low-level use of the program than high-level use. But in ASP the problems actually ran deeper than in SFA and AC. Much as detailed material resources were the linchpin of SFA, and much as professional education was the linchpin of AC, the transformation process was the linchpin of ASP. It was to function as the locus of school planning and development; as a model of the type of powerful, inquiry-oriented learning to be enacted in classrooms; as the context through which to effect change in school culture; and as the context within which to develop ASP's underlying philosophy. Yet, despite instances of success, many ASP schools struggled to enact the transformation process at even a base level. In 1997, ASP reported that, "although the inquiry process has been documented as representing a powerful strategy for improving schools . . . many schools have not found it easy to adopt and apply. Schools are typically not familiar with a systematic approach to decision-making, and they have difficulty in making it a regular part of their repertoire."[28]

A consequence of weak enactment of the transformation process was that change in culture, knowledge of ASP's philosophy, and understanding of powerful, inquiry-oriented learning were slow to emerge in ASP schools. They were slower yet to penetrate instructional practice. In 2000, internal research in one ASP satellite found great variation in teachers' use of powerful learning, even in schools thought to be high-implementing. Researchers reported that "the differences in implementation ratings may indicate a lack of a common understanding of, or commitment to, powerful learning among teachers within a school. It appears that teachers committed to and well versed in powerful learning teach side by side with teachers who either do not support the concept or have limited understanding of it."[29]

As with SFA and AC, ASP could have taken measures to establish conditions with potential to reduce the risk of problems while increasing
the possibility of success: for example, by cycling teachers and leaders
through high-functioning ASP schools as a means of acculturating them
to ASP; by eliminating instruction as a concern in order to focus exclu-
sively on school governance; by working only in districts supporting instructional practices consistent with notions of powerful learning; and/or
by accepting weak results as par for the course in high-poverty schools.
But, as with SFA and AC, ASP took schools as they were, advanced a comprehensive and ambitious design, worked in any and all environments,
and took responsibility for success.

Interactions: Schools and Environments

Where the AC design was predicated on weaknesses in schools and environments, the ASP design was predicated on latent and untapped strengths
in schools and environments. This is where ASP placed its chips. The task
was to identify, coordinate, and leverage these strengths to support school
and instructional improvement. Yet, in taking its design to practice, ASP
struggled to identify, coordinate, and leverage such strengths. But ASP's
problems also began with dysfunctional interactions among schools and
environments. And these interactions again created initial conditions fa-
voring low-level versus high-level enactment of the program.

The problems began with the system of satellites meant to function
as ASP's primary resource for recruiting schools and for supporting them
in enacting the transformation process. These satellites were fundamental to the ASP design. As argued by one senior ASP staff member,
"the project model alone was not enough to transform a school without
high quality training and ongoing coaching and implementation assistance."[30] Yet this system of satellites was composed of established, self-
funded organizations that functioned completely beyond the control of
ASP's National Center, such that the National Center had no say in such
essential matters as leadership, staffing, and operations.

Over its first decade, ASP succeeded in recruiting eleven satellites.
Again, these were organizations that existed in the proximal environments of ASP schools, and with which ASP schools may already have
had established relationships. In principle, all satellites would have the
capability to provide "consistent, high quality services, and capacity for
forward-thinking, proactive leadership versus reactive management."[31]
This approach was intended to build on strengths that already existed

in schools' environments, to increase the chances that schools would define their problems and solutions in ways that made local sense, and to increase the potential of institutionalizing ASP in established educational agencies and organizations.

One problem was that these satellites were indeed already going concerns, with their own leadership, agendas, operations, and constituencies. While ASP envisioned the potential to institutionalize the program in local educational organizations and agencies, the satellites' support for ASP schools was actually marginal to their missions and their operations. Simply put, ASP was not their core business.

Another problem was that, in addition to be being marginal to their missions and operations, the work that ASP expected of satellites was complex, novel, and typically beyond their existing capabilities. None of the satellites had prior knowledge of the ASP design, nor did they have coaches or other training staff with deep knowledge of how to best support the transformation process in schools. Moreover, where many had long experience providing conventional professional development to schools, few if any had knowledge and experience in collaborating with schools in multiyear capacity-building efforts.

Yet another problem was that, just as AC had weak leverage on districts, ASP had weak leverage on satellites. This was due in part to ASP's philosophical commitment to decentralization as a strategy for large-scale school improvement. ASP was committed to empowering schools and satellites to act on their own behalf while also cultivating their commitment to take responsibility for their own actions.[32] By the same token, commitment to decentralization kept them out of satellites' business. But ASP's weak leverage was also due to pragmatic considerations. ASP sought to capitalize on existing capabilities within the broader education system. All satellites were self-supporting and received no additional financial support from the National Center. The result was a weak foundation on which to begin building, with variation in the initial capabilities of satellites, the centrality of the program to their work, and their willingness to be coordinated by the National Center. Moreover, because ASP's National Center had weak leverage on satellites, it was a struggle to coordinate them in recruiting like-minded schools that understood and were willing to embrace ASP's core strategy.

Indeed, ASP scaled up its network of schools amid the same combination of policy-driven resources and pressures as SFA and AC. Absent careful recruitment and vetting by satellites, the results were familiar: large numbers of weak and turbulent schools that existed in weak and turbulent district and community environments. Many were weakly committed to improvement, having been drawn into comprehensive school reform primarily to access new funding streams. And many were weakly committed to Accelerated Schools, with some having adopted it because the lack of a detailed instructional design led them to perceive the program as requiring less work than other comprehensive school reform programs.[33]

Consequently, many ASP schools were weakly prepared to begin deep, comprehensive improvement absent extensive support from satellites. In that ASP was committed to taking schools as they were, these weaknesses became issues and problems that ASP's satellites had to manage. Indeed, satellites were a fundamental locus of coordination within the ASP design. Yet ASP's satellites varied in their capabilities and commitment to provide such assistance. In order to enact the transformation process as intended, all but the strongest satellites would have to develop new capabilities at the very same time that they worked to develop new capabilities in schools: first at a low level and then at a high level.

Interactions: Schools, Environments, and Design

Weak capabilities in schools and environments interacted to put pressure on the ASP design. In order to create the culture, philosophy, and understandings that would drive powerful learning in classrooms, schools and satellites needed support in coenacting the ASP transformation process. But, as with Success for All and America's Choice, the Accelerated Schools design did much more to support low-level use than high-level use. And, even with low-level use, the design created difficulties.

Contrary to schools' perceptions of Accelerated Schools as a path of least resistance, one problem was the sheer time and effort required to enact the transformation process.[34] The very foundation of Accelerated Schools was a commitment to slow, deep, and rich cultural transformation. Moreover, much of the work that SFA and AC did to guide instruction had to be done by schools themselves in the context of the ASP transformation process. That time and effort was often at odds with what ASP staff saw as a "quick fix" mentality in many US schools—a mentality that was exacerbated by increasing policy pressure to improve student achievement. As explained by ASP executives Christine Finnan and Henry Levin, the time and effort needed to enact the transformation process were at odds with school schedules that left little room for extended collaboration:

At its heart, the Accelerated School requires an internal transformation from standard operating procedures to active inquiry and problem-solving and from remediation to academic acceleration. But, such change is not magic. It entails considerable human endeavor for the training, practice, debate, discourse, deliberations, decisions, implementation, and evaluation. All of these activities require time in which both the full school staff and separate working groups can interact to undertake change in a systematic and responsive way. Unfortunately, most school schedules are not arranged to provide the time required for serious planning, preparation, and implementation.[35]

As with Success for All and America's Choice, another problem was that, owing to philosophical commitments to decentralization and practical constraints that came with operating a lean National Center, Accelerated Schools did not provide formal guidance with the detail that was needed to enact the program at a high level. This was the case for the transformation process. For example, the National Center did not provide detailed guidance for monitoring and assessing schools' performance, nor did it provide guidance for assessing satellites' support of schools in enacting the transformation process. This lack of detail was also the case for instructional practice. Though Accelerated Schools provided descriptions of powerful learning as an instructional design, an external evaluation found that school staffs "tended to report difficulties in understanding (and thus applying) the powerful learning framework in everyday instructional practice."[36] And this was the case for leadership practice too. As in Success for All and America's Choice, school leaders bore primary responsibility for school-level implementation.[37] However, Accelerated Schools offered leaders more encouragement than detailed guidance for practice. This was especially true for principals. While Accelerated Schools encouraged the inclusion of principals in the training for internal and external coaches, it did not offer training specifically for them.[38]

The problem of weak formal guidance extended beyond schools to satellites. Each satellite was already a self-supporting, going concern. As such, each had to figure out on its own how to meld ASP operations with its primary mission. However, ASP had no control over the operations of satellites. Moreover, it provided little guidance to satellites either for establishing operations or for interpreting and enacting the transformation process. In terms of operations, two national ASP leaders wrote that "ASP centers need to develop strategies for (satellite) operations in a five-year plan, addressing staffing, finances, expansion, training and technical assistance plans, evaluation, special projects, and the like."[39] In terms of interpreting and enacting the transformation process, the national office and satellites were a very broadly defined partnership, in which central steering was limited to an internal advisory board that met once a year. One long-time satellite leader observed that relationships within the federation resembled the incoherence in most schools. In such loose partnerships, satellites could operate, interpret, and use the intervention quite differently.[40]

Interactions: Schools, Environments, Design, and Organizations

Schools, environments, and the design interacted to place demands on the National Center to provide the support needed to enact the transformation process successfully. But these demands exceeded the capabilities of the National Center.

One problem was that, as in SFA and AC, the National Center was still maturing as an organization, and it was struggling to develop the systems needed to support its work and the work of the network. For example, by the early 2000s, the National Center had yet to develop systems that would enable it to track demographic and other information for the schools actively participating in the network, including such essential information as leader turnover, staff hours in training, or the cost of supporting the school. By 2000, in the midst of rapid and widely distributed recruiting practices, ASP staff members reported that ASP's database was out of date and invalid, and the number of active schools was unknown. Further, ASP had no consistent and formal means to assess either the quality of implementation in schools or the quality of support provided to schools by satellites. Indeed, the National Center had no central data on schools' implementation or development in relation to the model's benchmarks. Hence, there was no way to compare judgments about implementation, either to other judgments or to model standards.

Unlike SFA and AC, another problem for ASP was that the National Center experienced turbulence in its executive leadership. In 2000, Henry Levin left Stanford and stepped down as director of ASP.[41] Gene Chasin, a long-time worker in ASP and former school principal, took over as director. The same year, the National Center moved from Stanford University to the University of Connecticut. At that time, the National Center consisted of Chasin and two part-time staff members (as compared, e.g., to SFA's 250 researchers, developers, and staff members at its national headquarters, and the 250 members of its geographically distributed training organization). Funds for the National Center were very tight, and fiscal problems were acute.

Most problematic, though, was that the National Center was held hostage by its own philosophies. This was an organization committed to

decentralization and local empowerment. Its founders intentionally designed ASP's system of satellites in order to reduce the need to develop
a powerful, central organization with capabilities to provide support to
the full network of schools. Throughout years of implementation, national leaders expressed concern about uneven support for schools across
satellites. They recognized shortcomings in formal support for enacting
the transformation process. And they recognized the need for schools
to receive stronger training and coaching. Yet, even then, national leaders continued to insist that it was most crucial for the National Center
to continue to focus chiefly on beliefs, values, and assumptions.[42] Two
national leaders wrote of a proposal to begin quality assurance, but the
proposal was that satellites would assess themselves, using benchmarks
and other tools that the National Center proposed to develop.[43]

Result: Problems of Coherence and Capabilities

The result was, again, within-network incoherence that undermined the
development of capabilities: that is, dysfunctional interactions among
schools, environments, the design, and the National Center that resulted
in few instances of high-level use, many instances of low-level use, and
even some instances of non-use. Variability in use arose from interactions among a model that offered little detailed guidance for instruction, schools that had little capability, a lean central organization that
offered schools little direct support, and satellites that did not recruit or
support schools as ASP expected. One risk was that schools would interpret the transformation process as governance alone and not see that
powerful learning was much more than "just good teaching." Another
was that schools would not struggle to enact the transformation process
at all.

   One primary, underlying cause of this incoherence was ASP's commitment to decentralization, which delegated to schools and satellites
much of the responsibility both for enacting the transformation process
and developing school-specific instructional improvement initiatives. In
1999, the National Center published a paper that portrayed decentralization as a "double-edged sword." The National Center recognized that
decentralization fostered advantages, including innovation, ownership,
geographic reach, and the ability to capitalize on existing capabilities
without building a huge central office with national reach. But it also
recognized decentralization as fostering inconsistent adherence to the
program and weak capabilities in schools.[44] Adherence to the ASP ideas
and program were weak, satellites' quality control of school implemen-

tation was low, and the National Center had no way to do independent quality control. As recognized in a 1995 report, "employing a model that allows educators to build capacity locally—to implement the Accelerated Schools philosophy and process with limited oversight from the National Center—. . . means the project effectively gives up its ability to guarantee the consistency of the model."[45]

To be sure, the National Center called on satellites to adhere more closely to the model, to be more consistent in training, and to deepen capability. The response from the satellites was to call on the National Center to provide more support and assistance to satellites and schools.[46] Each called for more "capacity," more services, and more active participation from the other, but decentralization and a pervasive lack of capability meant that neither could do what the other wanted.

The National Center saw this problem as most acute in the two satellites with the most schools, one headquartered in a state department of education and the other headquartered in a university. One of the satellites had developed a state-wide infrastructure that included an ASP director based in the state education agency and offices at six state university campuses. Consistent with the vision of ASP founders, the satellite developed the ownership and operational capability that the National Center envisioned, and it shared the resources it created with the movement. Yet this satellite was a leading worry, both because its leader's intense engagement with ASP was inconsistent with the vision of ASP developers and because it refused to pay fees to support the National Center. Without provisions for arbitration in its formal agreement with satellites, differences with this large-scale satellite continued unresolved. The National Center placed the satellite on "probation" in 2002, but, consistent with ASP's decentralization, the satellite operated as if nothing had changed. Also consistent with decentralization, the National Center had no legal way to protect the ASP brand by decommissioning the satellite, nor did it have a means to control the quality of implementation. Consequently, the satellite that was on probation could thrive, while the National Center and the movement as a whole struggled.

Conclusion

As SFA, AC, and ASP moved into the late 1990s and early 2000s, the presenting problem was low level of change in practitioners' capabilities, owing to their difficulty learning to enact the designs' more ambitious features. Many teachers and school leaders interpreted Success for

All's highly specified reading program as though they should put it into practice mechanically. They found it easier to follow the directions than to understand and use the program as a path to more flexible and expert practice. Many teachers and school leaders in America's Choice schools enacted the instructional frameworks in broad strokes, though without using expert professional knowledge to design and enact instruction in ways responsive to students and standards. Similarly, many Accelerated Schools teachers were much more likely to implement formal steps to change governance and culture than to create powerful learning.

The deeper problem, though, was within-network incoherence. All three interveners experienced a common pattern of dysfunctional interactions among their schools, designs, organizations, and environmental relationships that undermined (rather than supported) the development of practitioners' capabilities. Schools and environments interacted to create initial conditions that challenged (rather than supported) high-level implementation. These schools and environments interacted with designs that, though in motion for over a decade, were actually still in their early stages of development. Each provided sufficient guidance and support to enable base levels of use of the most fundamental components. None provided sufficient guidance and support to realize expert use of program resources to achieve the highest levels of implementation. Schools, environments, and designs interacted to create pressure on the interveners' still-developing organizations to provide the additional guidance and support needed to transcend these dysfunctional interactions. And, in each case, the interveners' organizations exacerbated (rather than transcended) that dysfunction.

These problems might have been manageable if teachers, school leaders, and external trainers alike had had some grasp of the sort of expert, diagnostic instruction that the interveners sought. If so, all could have seen developers' intentions, and all could have seen the potential to enact the designs at the expert level intended by developers. But few teacher education programs emphasized such instruction, so few teachers in newly recruited schools would have been able to see those things, and few brought knowledge or experience that would allow them to reach high levels of mastery.[47] Likewise, few school leaders had professional preparation or experience in instructional leadership, and even fewer trainers had any professional preparation or experience assisting weak schools in pursuing such ambitious designs. Developers did not count on such capabilities. But, if they had existed, the signature problem of implementation experienced by all three interventions might have been

avoided. Because it was not avoided, interveners' designs for effecting coherence and capabilities at a large scale, in interaction with weak schools,
weak environments, and their developing organizations, laid the foundation for low-level use.

How, then, do we explain the common problems experienced by all
three interveners?

Had we studied only SFA, we probably would have attributed them
to its detailed specification, arguing that the very program features that
enabled the intervention to change teaching and improve learning also
limited its capacity for change. In that hypothetical, the implied remedy
would have been a less specified program, with more opportunities for
teachers to develop and use professional judgment. Yet, had we studied only AC, we probably would have attributed the problems to the
considerable openness of the design, the extensive room that it made
for professional judgment, and the lack of sufficient specification. The
implied remedy would have been a more specified design, with less room
for professional judgment. And had we studied only ASP, we probably
would have offered an even more forceful version of our response to a
hypothetical solo study of AC.

Do comparisons among the three alter our explanation?

Each program did encounter barriers to understanding and use that
were, at one level, specific to the program. Success for All's very specified
design was interpreted as if implementation was a matter of following
scripts mechanically, in part because those scripts were the most promi-
nent feature of the design and thus easy for weak teachers to attend to.
America's Choice presented a much more open design, which required
that teachers learn the knowledge and skills that would enable them to
use instructional frameworks for reading and writing. It was much easier
to put the formal features of those frameworks into practice than to learn
the knowledge and skills that would enable effective use of the formal elements. Like Success for All's scripts, the formal elements were much more
accessible cognitively and were readily used in practice. In each case, to
understand and use the designs to achieve more expert practice required
understanding and practices that most teachers lacked.

If that is roughly correct, though, it implies that all three programs
shared a common vulnerability to superficial implementation. Moreover,
they experienced this common vulnerability despite their different core
strategies; despite their different attempts to structure functional relationships among schools, designs, environments, and their organizations; and
despite intervention-specific manifestations of weak implementation.

How can we explain that?

All three attempted fundamental change in America's weakest schools, despite the lack of an educational infrastructure that would support instruction and its improvement. Practitioners in the United States do not work with a common curriculum that is referenced to common examinations, and they do not have professional education that is grounded in learning to teach that curriculum. The presence of such an infrastructure is no guarantee of good instruction. It still must be designed and used well to be effective. But the absence of such an infrastructure means that if US schools are to develop quality instructional programs, they cannot use what already exists. Instead, they must devise an infrastructure themselves, and find ways to sustain it over time through changes in management, policy, and politics. That is difficult to accomplish even in advantaged schools and systems, and much more so in high-poverty schools. It is an important reason why very few of those schools had substantial instructional programs.

This situation meant that the interveners' task was, quite literally, systemic change: to invent strong programs of instruction; to find ways to bring them to weak schools; to devise organizations that could help practitioners learn to use those programs effectively, and to do these things absent much support from the environment. In that circumstance, deep problems in changing practices and understandings were unavoidable. The "meta" design task was quite literally to invent systems of schooling. Yet the interveners could never set out anything close to an exhaustive set of all the things that practitioners would need to know and do. They would always fall short of what they could have covered and needed to cover. Similarly, help with implementation could never offer anything close to the professional education that would be required. It, too, would always be partial. And even with the best design and most useful help with implementation, practitioners always would have so much to learn that their practice would need to improve over very long periods of time if it were to rise to the level of the interveners' intentions.

The interventions' systemic qualities were a strength and a weakness. They spanned teaching, leadership, environments, and organization. That enabled coordinated improvement in many related aspects of schools. But it also transformed implementation into a complex puzzle that required managing interactions among schools, designs, organizations, and environments. The systemic interventions increased the chance that problems in using one part of a design would ripple through to others, putting the entire enterprise at risk. The more systemic the intervention, the more problems it engaged, including weak instruction, student mobility, classroom discipline, parents' involvement, teachers' weak education, and teacher mobility. Yet the more problems a design engaged, the more work it made for the developers, trainers, and practitioners. The more aspects of schooling an intervener sought to improve, the more elements of the environment with which it came into contact. The more such contacts there were, the more opportunities for conflict there were, either between guidance from interventions and environments, or between guidance from different agencies in the environment. The systemic interventions helped SFA and AC to succeed, for they provided the crucial advantage of technical infrastructure, but they also led to large problems of coordination in the designs and in schools' use of them.

Even if the interveners had created error-free designs, the sorts of implementation puzzles discussed in this chapter would be part of any conceivable change process. From this perspective, the key difference among the interventions was how their designs, organizations, and guiding ideas equipped them to deal with such unavoidable problems. AC and SFA had several advantages. They had designs for instruction. Though many practitioners did not use them at nearly the level the developers intended, they used them, which was a plain improvement on the existing instruction. They built organizations that could support schools' use of the designs. As a result, a large fraction of their schools saw change in teaching and improvement in learning. Their central organizations were staffed by educators who observed implementation, noted problems, and advised about changes in designs and support for implementation. Moreover, both AC and SFA were committed to using evidence from professional observation and research to improve the designs and implementation. That was a distinctly mixed blessing. Dismaying evidence about the problems that arose from the ambitious designs' use in weak schools fed back to the interventions, and made much more work and worry for them. Yet AC and SFA had some of the resources they needed to interpret the evidence, revise the designs, and improve assistance to schools.

ASP had few of these advantages. Its design was as open as it was ambitious, and it required very demanding work from schools. There was a very modest design for instruction, and the decentralized operations meant that implementation support depended on agencies whose chief missions were elsewhere and that received no resources beyond revenue from school contracts to support their work. Decentralization also meant that the National Center lacked both the human resources to closely monitor implementation and the political influence to act on implementation problems. The design was much better suited to use by schools that brought appreciable capability to the work. Accelerated Schools was used effectively in a small number of schools, but it did not have the broad average effects across many schools evidenced by Success for All and America's Choice.

Given the weaknesses in schools and the environment that we discussed, the success that SFA and AC had in schools is remarkable testimony to the designs and the work that the interveners did to help schools. But these effects were not all that their founders had intended. The problems that all three interveners encountered are equally remarkable testimony to the difficulty of improving schools that have many weaknesses, in environments that offer little help and many obstacles, when the interveners had, in addition to their designs, only the organizations that they could build, the private money they could raise, and the schools' willingness to spend their effort and federal Title I funds to improve teaching and learning. That schools improved *at all*, on any level, was a major achievement. But for all three interveners, it remained to be determined whether they could correct the problems discussed here in pursuit of their higher ambitions.

The Improvement Puzzle

By the early 2000s, SFA, AC, and ASP were staring down complex implementation puzzles: unforeseen dynamics among schools, their designs, their organizations, and environments. These dynamics had many schools engaged in low levels of use, far fewer schools advancing to higher levels of use, and large numbers of students achieving below desired levels.

Further, they were staring down these puzzles amid turbulence in educational environments, broader environments, and the interactions between them. In educational environments, the passage of No Child Left Behind (NCLB) appeared to increase not only system-wide resources and incentives to improve the technical effectiveness of schools. It also increased the resources and incentives supporting comprehensive school reform as one means of doing so. At the same time, one of the chief boosters and patrons of the comprehensive school reform movement—the New American Schools initiative—was winding down. Further, the broader economic downturn that resulted from the bursting of the dot-com bubble reduced philanthropic investment in education reform, and the attacks of September 11, 2001, dramatically altered the national policy agenda in ways that would soon draw attention and resources away from education reform.

Just as the interveners' design puzzle led to the implementation puzzle, the implementation puzzle led to the improvement puzzle: the need to intervene on their self-constructed systems to improve practice and outcomes in district-sized and state-sized networks of schools operating in complex and turbulent environments. But the implementation puzzle was not theirs alone. Indeed, under NCLB's increased pressure for technical effectiveness, districts and states were encountering the improvement puzzle themselves.

There was a deep irony to all of this. On the one hand, few districts and states had ever seriously engaged such work, and few had capabilities to support it. Yet districts and states benefited from institutionalized funding, formal authority, and new funding streams to support such work. On the other hand, SFA, ASP, and AC were founded precisely to engage such work, and they were developing formidable capabilities to support it. Yet the three interveners did so absent institutionalized funding, formal authority, and stable philanthropic contributions.

Even so, in the early 2000s the interveners did not perceive any sort of existential threat that would render them yesterday's news—at least not yet. Rather, they saw new opportunity. For the leaders of SFA and AC, viability seemed a sure thing, with continued growth and long-term operations functioning as assumptions. While the leaders of ASP began to acknowledge concerns about a potential clash between its strategy and the demands of NCLB, they continued to anticipate opportunities to establish partnerships with large numbers of like-minded schools that sought to leverage cultural change as a foundation for instructional improvement.

With expectations for continued growth, a sensible conjecture would be that increasing pressure for technical effectiveness would have driven SFA, ASP, and AC into a pattern of conventional, rational problem solving: study the problem; develop or acquire the knowledge needed to solve it; fashion and pilot solutions; disseminate those solutions; and initiate large-scale implementation. After all, this is precisely the four-phase structure that New American Schools had used to structure the work of its design teams. Moreover, projecting this sort of rationality is precisely what many do to inspire confidence, maintain legitimacy, and secure resources under conditions of turbulence and uncertainty. And, again, absent institutionalized funding, formal authority, and stable philanthropic contributions, such things as inspiring confidence, maintaining legitimacy, and securing resources were high on the interveners' "to do" lists.

However, in no case does our evidence support the interpretation that the interveners engaged the improvement puzzle through conventional, rational problem solving, and for all of the reasons that have long limited (if not undermined) rationality in organizations and in policy making.

The problems at hand were not clear, nor was the array of possible solutions, the interactions among them, the means of accurately forecasting implementation and effects in schools, or the criteria for selecting among the lot. Indeed, the interveners were overwhelmed with information from classrooms, schools, and environments, and they were unsure of how exactly to prioritize and process the information to identify patterns of problems in schools. They were operating amid weak knowledge of instructional and school improvement and still weaker knowledge of how to structure and manage their own organizations. And they were operating amid environmental uncertainty that had unpredictable implications for designs, schools, and their own organizations. Indeed, the disconnect between interveners' well-reasoned designs and their subsequent implementation puzzles stands as evidence of the challenge of bringing rationality to bear on the goal of increasing capabilities and coherence at scale.

Instead, our evidence supports the interpretation that SFA, ASP, and AC engaged the improvement puzzle in ways that many others have used to solve complex problems amid limited rationality and environmental turbulence: they muddled through. Moreover, their muddling exhibited a similar pattern across the three interveners. Continuously, all three interveners worked to interpret large volumes of information from schools and from broader environments, much generated and communicated informally by their own training staffs. Based on their ongoing interpretation of this information, they engaged in divergent activity in which they experimented with systemic improvements in their designs, schools, organizations, and environmental relationships; converged on promising improvements; and quickly began enacting them network-wide. That, in turn, evoked new interactions among design, schools, their organizations, and environments (some favorable and many problematic), which drove further muddling.[1]

Indeed, for all three interveners, to engage the improvement puzzle was to engage the design and implementation puzzles constantly, simultaneously, and in interaction in ways that drove continuous improvement through concurrent action, reflection, and adaptation. We cannot overstate the complexity and urgency of this activity, nor the extensive capabilities and resources brought to bear. At the same time, we cannot overstate the limitations of trying to capture these dynamics in conventional, sequential text.

We continue, then, by providing a summary of the efforts of SFA, ASP, and AC to engage the improvement puzzle through the early 2000s, full well recognizing that we forgo reporting important details in order to report broad patterns. The broadest of those patterns is, by now, familiar: even with well-reasoned and interdependent improvements in their schools, their designs, their own organizations, and their interactions with environments, all three interveners again occasioned and experienced unanticipated interactions among them.

Yet in these unanticipated interactions lie the more difficult puzzles of cyclical, evolutionary, continuous improvement. These unanticipated interactions did not only recommence (and further complicate) the design and implementation puzzles. Despite initial, optimistic assumptions about new opportunities under NCLB, they also risked undermining the continued viability of their own interventions.

Accelerated Schools

By the late 1990s and early 2000s, ASP's version of the implementation puzzle was that schools succeeding in enacting the design were often doing so at only a low level: for example, by creating new roles and structures, enacting the steps of the transformation process, and improving the cultures of their schools. However, few were succeeding in leveraging ASP's transformation process to effect powerful learning in classrooms. Within ASP, this pattern of implementation was understood to be the consequence of three interdependent problems: design weaknesses in bridging from cultural transformation to instructional improvement; variable and weak implementation support from ASP's external satellite partners; and weak quality control in ASP's National Center.

As ASP began recognizing problems of implementation, it reprised the design puzzle, with the goal of adapting its schools, designs, organization, and environmental relations to increase the potential for technical effectiveness. In the spring of 2003, Gene Chasin, the director of ASP's National Center, drew on emerging understandings to communicate a vision for a new direction for ASP, and he invited all satellite directors to participate in shaping and enacting that vision.[2] The goal was to preserve the culture- and process-based design for schools while providing substantially improved (and more consistent) support for implementation.[3]

While successful in many ways, enacting this new vision for ASP also reoccasioned the implementation puzzle. Improvements in the enterprise evoked interactions that created new threats to technical effectiveness. At the same time, environmental turbulence created new threats to continued viability.

ASP: Reprise—the Design Puzzle

ASP's improvement efforts centered on restructuring the enterprise to include more centralization and standardization of training and implementation support. This included efforts to be more selective in recruiting schools, to increase instructional support within the ASP design, to strengthen the National Center to improve support for implementation, and to reduce the operational demands on autonomous external partners.

Schools

As part of its efforts to drive the transformation process into classrooms, ASP devised three means of ensuring that schools were strongly committed to the program. With conviction and ownership still seen as the foundation for effective implementation, the first was to develop a formal buy-in process to be coenacted by prospective schools and ASP trainers. For schools, the aim was to clarify the ASP design and its demands on leaders, teachers, and students. For ASP, the aim was to assess the authenticity of buy-in as a condition for accepting or rejecting schools. Also new to ASP, the buy-in process was extended to districts, with the requirement that districts formally commit to supporting implementation. Lastly, in contrast to earlier agreements between schools and ASP's regional satellites, the buy-in process included a formal contract between schools and the National Center.

The second means of ensuring the strong commitment of schools was by developing a formal implementation assessment process. Instead of schools assessing themselves, ASP training staff would administer an instrument that incorporated but did not rely on schools' self-assessments.[4] Continuation was contingent on quality of implementation. ASP would not renew the contracts of schools deemed not to be implementing or not making a good-faith attempt.

The third means of ensuring the strong commitment of schools was to develop an incentive system through which excellent implementers would be invited to apply to be designated as national demonstration sites. Besides motivating commitment in individual schools, the idea was that working models would help other schools to understand how the design was supposed to work and how they might make it work for themselves. National demonstration sites would open their doors to staff in other ASP schools, and principals from the model schools would participate in central network or training sessions for staff from other schools.[5] The national demonstration sites were seen as key to reorienting schools away from the idea of quick fixes and toward the idea of long-term, deep-reaching improvement. As explained by one ASP executive in a 2004 interview, "what we had to do was make sure we had schools that represented [to newer schools] that capacity building was the prime engine driving school improvement."[6]

Design

In considering design improvements, ASP leaders found themselves needing to manage a tension. On the one hand, they knew that schools needed more specific guidance about the nature of powerful learning, how it fit within the model, and how to implement it. On the other hand, they were deeply disinclined either to prescribe practice or to pull back from their commitment to process-focused change.

ASP's strategy for managing this tension centered on three core design improvements. The first was to codify a menu of instructional strategies for use in schools. The purpose was not to preclude schools from using the transformation process to devise their own action plans. Rather, the aim was to support a sort of "learning by doing" that would have schools enacting powerful learning and learning from experience at the very same time that they enacted the transformation process.[7] Rather than discussing the idea of powerful learning as a distant goal to be pursued once schools had begun to transform, schools were now to begin using the sample strategies to enact powerful learning in the first year of implementation. With that, teachers would have first-hand, shared, and continuing experience with powerful learning immediately on beginning implementation, as well as with its links to cultural change and the transformation process.

The second design improvement was to provide schools with more specific implementation benchmarks. The goal was to be more precise about both what implementation of cultural change would involve and what cultural change would look like in instruction. The benchmarks provided specific criteria that could be used by schools to examine the extent to which the ASP governance structure supported the development and implementation of acceleration and powerful learning. For example, the benchmarks encouraged schools to examine the extent to which students demonstrated learning through the creation of authentic products and performances; the extent to which teachers continuously gathered evidence of student learning in order to adjust and modify instruction;

and the extent to which learning was accelerated by differentiating instruction to meet students' needs, interests, and strengths.[8]

The third design improvement was to provide stronger and more consistent support for school leaders in supporting implementation. This included more extensive elaboration of formal leadership practices that focused on supporting teachers in understanding and using ASP-supplied resources. As important, it included more extensive and consistent practice-based learning opportunities for school leaders. This included an annual "Leadership Academy" training held each fall at the University of Connecticut, which was complemented by local, regional, and national networking opportunities. It also include restructuring of ASP's coaching model to include eighteen days per year of school-based support from ASP trainers, one component of which had ASP trainers mentoring school leaders in observing and coaching teachers.

Besides providing increased support for schools, these changes also had potential to provide ASP with information about each school's progress, including patterns of participation across faculty members and classrooms. This information would have ASP trainers more strongly positioned to troubleshoot in response to each school's needs. It would also enable continuity in the school in the face of principal turnover, district leadership changes, and more. The combination of improved information and continuity could help to offset institutional turbulence that had undermined implementation in the past.

Organizations

Improvements in schools and the design were matched with efforts to strengthen the National Center, both to standardize and improve support and to assess (and ensure) quality implementation. The National Center maintained many of its previous operations. For example, it administered an annual customer satisfaction survey, maintained and developed the website and bimonthly newsletter, lobbied state and federal agencies, and represented ASP throughout the United States.

However, the National Center initiated a radical change that greatly reduced its dependence on environments: it moved training support from independent regional satellites to newly created "provider centers." While still in different institutional hosts, ASP's new provider centers operated in tight relationships with the National Center. The staff of provider centers (called "national faculty") would be employed by the National Center's institutional host, the University of Connecticut. Rather than at the discretion of satellites, national faculty would be hired by the National Center based on their knowledge of ASP's ideas and school design, their teaching experience, and their effectiveness in work with schools.[9] National faculty would hold contracts with the National Center, they would be paid by the National Center, and they would serve as at-will employees who would be evaluated (and could be fired) every year based on performance. National faculty reported to a provider center director, who reported to a regional director, who reported to the director of the National Center.

As it established and staffed provider centers, ASP also standardized support for the professional development and practice of national faculty. Key professional development opportunities included two weeks of training at the University of Connecticut, which was complemented by school-based modeling and mentoring. Key supports for the practice of national faculty included a standardized assessment instrument used both to focus site visits and to determine the continued participation of schools based on quality of implementation.

Especially important was a more specified, common design for school-based support. In contrast to each satellite devising its own implementation support around a suggested set of topics (e.g., "powerful learning" or "the inquiry process"), all national faculty were to implement standard training modules with full school faculties within a subset of the eighteen on-site school training days.[10] The modules set out learning goals, key questions and content, and sample activities, and they also supported discovery learning opportunities for teachers and school leaders. As described at one ASP training session, "we aim to practice what we preach. Training should be powerful learning."[11]

As the National Center asserted new control, it also created new structures for movement-wide governance and operations, with the aim of distributing responsibilities and leadership throughout the organization, improving knowledge flow, and reinforcing the mission. Beyond school-based support, national faculty were responsible for developing materials for use in schools. They also participated in agenda setting, governance, and problem solving through regularly scheduled phone meetings, biweekly cadre meetings, and a biweekly conference call for the movement as a whole. A steering committee, comprised of National Center director Chasin and national faculty, met by phone every other week. Chasin explained that efforts to distribute leadership and responsibility were intended to further strengthen the ASP organization:

We're building on the strengths of everyone in the organization now. . . . That was not the case before. We are being informed by the people who are most directly working with the schools. They have as much voice as I do in the development efforts, and they should. . . . There's unity within the organization, and there's a shared vision, and all those pieces that we espouse to schools is in place and modeled within the faculty. The hierarchy doesn't exist.[12]

Though more elaborate, this was still a lean operation. Initially there were three regional directors, seven provider centers and directors, about twenty national faculty members.[13] Staffing at the National Center also remained lean, with only three employees in 2004.[14]

Environments

While ASP's shift to provider centers greatly reduced dependence on satellite organizations in its environment, the National Center continued to rely on agencies in its environment for assistance and support. For example, each provider center had institutional hosts that had potential to add value to the enterprise, including the Center for Gifted and Talented Education in the Neag School of Education at the University of Connecticut. Further, the National Center formed an external advisory board to make useful connections in the environment. The board included members with academic, business, and policy expertise, with the aim of the board being to provide strategic advice in such domains as marketing and policy analysis.[15] Finally, ASP joined a consortium of "process-based" school improvement models. As explained by ASP director Chasin, the goals were both to connect with and gain support from organizations that shared values:

There is significantly more communication and collaboration happening between the process-based models like ELOB (Experiential Learning/Outward Bound), Atlas, Accelerated Schools, Co-NECT. It's significant. I don't know that we ever viewed ourselves as competitors, but we never have seen so much mutual support for the models, and that's been an exciting development. . . . We have many shared components and we have common shared needs. For example, we're doing work with data analysis and data training for schools collaboratively. . . . There is a federal grant that we've gotten to put together both a data system for school districts, but also training for our schools in how to mine and utilize data.[16]

ASP: Reprise—the Implementation Puzzle

These improvement initiatives greatly increased the potential for ASP schools to move beyond organizational and cultural improvement to instructional improvement. In a 2007 interview, one ASP executive reported that "the shift of focus to the classroom and teaching and learning behaviors has resulted in much more rapid implementation. And people understand the purpose for all the cultural and governance shifts that we make, because the instructional practice serves as the lens for it."[17]

These improvements were not only the product of more extensive elaboration of ASP's ideals and processes but also ASP's efforts to provide more consistent and focused professional education. Indeed, Chasin explained that an early pilot of ASP's new model for school-based support "yielded greatly increased implementation . . . and resulted in increased achievement in a much shorter time span than with the previous coaching model."[18] More engaged and effective schools, finally, had potential to sustain ASP's ambitions for deep and lasting improvement in the face of increasing policy pressure for rapid increases in standardized test scores.

Even so, simultaneous improvements in schools, the design, the National Center, and its environmental relationships had the effect of introducing new and compounding problems among them. The result was to leave the identity and continued viability of ASP in question.

Interactions—Organizations and Environments

The problems began with interactions between ASP's efforts to strengthen its central organization and its long-standing relationship with the free-standing, independent educational organizations that functioned as the mission-critical satellites. While the new approach reflected input from satellite leaders over several years, the shift to ASP-managed provider centers from independent satellites resulted in four of eleven satellites declining the invitation to participate as provider centers. This included the two satellites that accounted for the majority of ASP's participating schools. This schism was rooted in a perceived cultural shift that went with moving ASP from a loose federation of organizations to a more centralized system. It was also rooted in objections to the actual design of this more centralized system.

Making matters worse, the loss of four satellites also compromised the ASP brand. In constructing the former loose federation among satellites and the National Center, the National Center had never taken measures to secure ownership of ASP as brand. As such, the satellites who rejected the restructuring still had rights to the brand.

As a result, the National Center had to identify a new name for the reorganized ASP. Specifically, the National Center and the new provider centers elected to change their name to Accelerated Schools Plus (AS Plus) to distinguish themselves and to establish a brand and identity distinct from the "ASP" brand still used by the ex-satellites.

Interactions—Organizations, Environments, and Schools

New problems in the interactions between the organization and its environments were compounded by new problems with schools. To start, the decision of four satellites not to participate in AS Plus resulted in a dramatic drop in the installed base of schools. Having peaked at 1,400 schools with some affiliation with ASP, AS Plus identified 200 schools that had active contracts with the National Center.[19]

National Center leaders saw an upside to the reduction in scale, in that they saw a smaller set of more committed schools as creating opportunity for a more like-minded and committed group of educators to improve both implementation and outcomes. As one ASP executive explained in a 2003 interview, "Smaller is better in terms of maintaining quality."[20]

Even so, the reduction in its scale of operations decreased the potential for AS Plus to have a large national influence on education. Indeed, the nonaffiliated satellites continued to operate with the prior design under the name of the Accelerated Schools Project, with a total count of schools potentially higher than that of AS Plus.

Interactions—Organizations, Environments, Schools, and Design

Even with a smaller and more committed group, improvements in the AS Plus design did not make the work of these 200 schools any easier. To start, schools had to identify means of funding the adoption of the new design improvements. Though AS Plus was providing much more support, the cost to schools was twice what it had been in the late 1990s.

Further, even for those schools able to find funding, the design improvements did not fundamentally alter the demands of enacting the program. Since AS Plus remained committed to its process-based design and to cultural transformation, it still depended on schools to devise ways to link cultural transformation with instructional improvement. AS Plus's new sample instructional strategies could help. However, they were far from a curriculum, and they were not intended to replace each school's use of inquiry to analyze its problems and figure out the solutions that made most sense for it.[21] At a network meeting in 2004 attended by more than a hundred school professionals, when asked to identify their "burning questions," an old theme emerged: school staff still expressed the need for help in using AS Plus's ideas and philosophies to improve instruction.[22]

The continued demands of the design interacted with changing environments to further increase the problems faced by schools. The first problem was the matter of time. The passage of NCLB in 2001 created pressure on all US public schools (especially underperforming, high-poverty schools) to quickly demonstrate adequate yearly progress (AYP) toward state standards for student achievement, on average and across subgroups of students. The second problem was that NCLB limited conceptions of school improvement. The press to demonstrate AYP toward state standards greatly narrowed the room available for schools and external interveners to determine for themselves the aims and methods of school improvement.

That put AS Plus and its schools in a difficult position. On the point of time, the designers were confident that, if schools implemented the design well, they would see improved achievement. However, they also believed it would take about five years to see those improvements. But NCLB pressured schools to demonstrate progress on an annual basis. On the point of limiting conceptions of school improvement, AS Plus was about much more than test scores. There was broad concern among designers that the intensifying focus on high-stakes tests narrowed the curriculum and detracted from student ownership of learning, which AS Plus saw as a necessary foundation for authentic and long-term student achievement. It also undermined the effort to enable each school to build its own cultural identity, to identify its own problems and goals, and to chart a course for solving those problems and pursuing those goals.

AS Plus schools that were considering or had adopted the design thus were caught in precisely the ideological battle that its leaders had begun to anticipate on the reauthorization of NCLB. State and federal policy placed great weight on rapid improvement in test scores, but AS Plus saw the environment's "clear preference for prescriptive models" and a "narrowing of the curriculum" as antithetical to their design.[23] As explained by ASP executives:

The pressures of compliance with standardization and testing practices demanded by states and districts diverts teacher efforts to create powerful learning environments. In many cases, ASP schools must meet two sets of standards, their own and those of government authorities, [creating] a strain on school personnel and other resources.[24]

That was especially difficult for schools that had adopted AS Plus or that were considering it, since, in many states, adoption would be seen as opposition to prevailing policies and educational values, perhaps including those of the school's own district. That would have been much less of a problem in 1975, when few state or federal policies challenged local control. But in the age of NCLB, state and federal policies pressed schools to conform to the practices that tests, standards, and accountability represented. AS Plus renewed its emphasis that practitioners understand its ideas and use them to make cultural change that improved teaching and learning, because those ideas were what distinguished AS Plus from the environment. But those ideas were more difficult for schools to adopt and operationalize than ever.

Problems in the interactions among the design, schools, and especially environments fed back onto the organization. One problem was in funding all of these initiatives in a difficult economic climate, in an organization not able to operate on deficit spending. Another problem was in the sheer demands on the time and energy of AS Plus staff members. When AS Plus and its provider centers took more responsibility, there was more for them to do, in an environment that offered less support and more opposition than there had been just a few years earlier. Yet there was not enough time to do the work, given the organization's fiscal and human resources. The result, explained Chasin, was tremendous stress on the people in the organization.

People in the organization . . . have such deep commitment to the model. They are working themselves to death. I don't think anyone on our team would ever give a thought to leaving. I'm not worried about that. I'm worried about the burn-out issue though. Because of the degree of communication and development work that's going on, the workload significantly increased for field staff.[25]

The rebranded AS Plus made significant progress on several fronts, but these improvements made much more work for the entire organization, and they occurred in an environment that was less open to long-term improvement initiatives intended to deeply transform inherited ideas, practices, and organizations. In that sense, AS Plus walked a tightrope, as it tried to balance competing influences and aspirations. It needed support from the environment to sustain schools' work and to recruit new schools, but it also needed to declare its independence from the dominant environment of testing and accountability. It needed more central direction for implementation, but it also needed even more dedicated participation from its staff and those in schools. It needed field staff in its provider centers to work even harder, but it also needed them to work more consistently with each other and the National Center. It needed more professional knowledge and skill to improve schools' implementation, but it also needed to insist on the centrality of cultural change and schools' decisions about how to solve their problems.

These contrary pressures reflected increasing tension between ASP's founding ideas and ideas prevailing under NCLB. That tension, in turn, raised serious questions about the viability of ASP in NCLB-affected environments.

Success for All

As its version of the implementation problem came to a head in the late 1990s, SFA leaders and developers began pooling reports from schools and trainers with their own observations. With that, they were quick to interpret implementation problems as having roots in the design itself: specifically, its extensive elaboration of and emphasis on novice practice, and its comparatively weak elaboration of and emphasis on expert practice. Members of SFA were slower to recognize that its own trainers were exacerbating these problems. They were slower yet to recognize that the trainers' problems had still deeper roots in its systems that supported the work and professional development of trainers. These interpretations reflected SFA's orientation toward and extensive experience with external designs as resources for school improvement, as well as its comparative inexperience designing and managing large, complex organizations.

These interpretations fueled an urgent improvement cycle that ran from 1999 to 2003. As with AS Plus, SFA pursued evolutionary improvements in its strategy for recruiting schools, its design, the organization, and its relationship with its environments. And as with AS Plus, the results were new potential for success, new threats to implementation, and new threats to continued viability.

SFA: Reprise—the Design Puzzle

SFA's improvement cycle had two primary goals, both of which were tied to coordinated changes in its schools, designs, organization, and environmental relationships. The first was to develop capabilities in teachers and leaders for more expert and more coordinated use of the design. The second was to position SFA for continued scale-up amid new opportunities under NCLB, both by adapting to and attempting to influence its environments.

Schools

SFA began with considering how best to manage its network of schools. This was no simple matter. Over the 1990s, rapid recruitment of large numbers of weak schools had exacerbated SFA's design problems. Teachers and school leaders weak in initial capabilities were quick to interpret and use the program either as a bureaucratic implement or a technocratic quick fix, and few had the knowledge and capabilities to support expert use of the design.

However, rather than solving such problems by slowing down the pace of recruitment and reducing the size of the network, SFA sought to sustain its pace of recruitment and to further expand the network. In the late 1990s and early 2000s, SFA's leaders began to see potential in NCLB to further institutionalize the comprehensive school reform movement, both through continued support for whole-school reform under Title I and by incorporating the Obey-Porter Comprehensive School Reform Demonstration Program under the umbrella of NCLB.

SFA executives projected that, if successful in using the 1999–2003 improvement cycle to align its programs with new requirements and opportunities under NCLB, expansion to 2,000 schools was a sure thing, and expansion to 3,000 schools was a very real possibility. Such growth had potential to further raise SFA's profile in the national educational reform community. Further, for an organization whose financial strategy was highly dependent on new business, such growth was also critical for generating the operating capital that SFA need to further establish and solidify its own organization.

Design

SFA continued with its primary source of comparative advantage: its design for learning, teaching, and leadership. SFA's experience under Obey-Porter had reinforced its founding belief in the strength of comprehensive school reform, both as a solution for schools and a market niche in which it could flourish and possibly dominate. As such, SFA's design improvements were corrections to and incremental expansions of what seemed a solid foundation.

Among the initial design improvements was an effort to develop language and resources that could be used to help schools frame and interpret SFA not as bureaucratic or technocratic but, instead, as a resource supporting evidence-driven practice, learning, and improvement.

This effort yielded three frameworks: the "change process," which was used to describe implementation as a school-wide, multiyear growth process; the "levels of use" framework, which was used to describe eight distinct stages through which teachers' practice would progress en route from novice to expert; and the "stages of concern" framework, which described affective and emotional stages through which teachers would progress en route from novice to expert.[26] The frameworks made very clear distinctions between "routine" (or novice) and "refined" (or expert) use of the program, misinterpretation of which had been at the heart of weak implementation. The frameworks became key resources for school leaders and trainers in managing teachers' interpretation and use of the design.[27]

SFA continued by developing an extensive array of resources and training opportunities aimed at supporting expert use of the program. For teachers, SFA standardized the language of expert use across curriculum components, improved support for formative assessment and subsequent instructional adaptations, and represented expert use by embedding video and DVD technology in classroom instruction. The 1999–2003 improvement cycle also placed a particularly keen focus on new resources for school leaders, the absence of which had long been a weakness within the program. These included new routines, information resources, and guidance to support analysis of implementation and effectiveness across the program, using both internal program data and results from state accountability assessments. They included routines and guidance to align the program with state standards and assessments. They included a curriculum (the Building Better Readers series) for use by school leaders in supporting teachers' practice-based learning. And they included a sort of metaroutine—the Goal-Focused Improvement Process—that integrated these elements into a continuous improvement cycle for teachers and leaders.

SFA also improved professional education by supporting use of the new resources. That included yearly revisions to the standard initial training for all schools (to emphasize and support the change from routine to refined implementation); changes in implementation visits to avoid overemphasis on fidelity and to include analyses of instructional processes and outcomes; and annual increases and improvements in learning opportunities for leaders and teachers in conferences and school-based training. Especially important were efforts to strengthen the Success for All network through the creation of monthly Leadership Academy sessions for neighboring schools, which included practice-based, school-specific assistance to school leaders in using new program resources to analyze and respond to implementation and achievement problems.

Organizations

SFA's focus on improving the design, combined with its success in raising soft money to support such work, drove a rapid expansion in the in-house development organization. It grew large and complex, and included development capability for curriculum, assessment, leadership, software, and media production, along with capability to expand into pre-K and middle school. SFA hired staff with extensive expertise in program improvement, including expert users of Success for All, and it established productive relationships with development organizations in its environment, including commercial testing and media production firms.

The increase in size and complexity in the development organization was matched with new urgency in its work. The urgency was driven in part by SFA's mission to do as much as possible to serve students. The lives of real children hung in the balance, which led developers to try to help them by rapidly devising improvements. The urgency was also driven by pressure on schools to improve achievement that, in turn, had them putting pressure on SFA for program improvements. Successful response to this pressure would demonstrate Success for All's effectiveness but, by the same token, failure to respond potentially exposed the program's limitations. And finally, the urgency was driven by the environment. As SFA executives looked forward to NCLB, they expected it to bring new opportunity for growth and more pressure on schools to boost achievement.

Growth in the development organization came with some structural formalization, including the creation of new departments and roles. However, SFA's executives did not match the size and complexity of the development organization with efforts to coordinate its work using formal methods and procedures for project management. Instead, the SFA development organization continued to operate as a research-and-development shop. Design improvements were coordinated largely informally, among members of different development teams and through SFA executives who were the hubs of SFA's social networks.

SFA's informality was a resource for rapid, distributed experiential learning and urgent, distributed design improvement. Dense, informal relationships moved information, understanding, and ideas quickly within the organization, and they provided unusual support to rapidly improve the program while working at a large scale.

Environments

Throughout the 1999–2003 improvement cycle, SFA took aggressive action to manage its relationship with environments to support its development efforts, to increase potential for expert use, and, especially, to position itself for continued scale-up. Continued scale-up was important. It promised better education for more students, it would strengthen SFA's network of schools, and it would provide necessary revenue for the central organization.

Toward those ends, SFA continued to succeed in securing funds to support its development initiatives. Further, it continued to monitor the environment to identify new knowledge about program improvement (e.g., the ideas of the National Reading Panel) and to identify new technologies (e.g., commercial tests). Finally, it continued work in Washington to shape conditions that would favor the continued growth of comprehensive school reform in general and SFA in particular. For example, SFA executives continued to advocate for the use of scientifically based research in program development and evaluation, and they lobbied and testified in the reauthorization hearings leading up to the passage of NCLB.

The organization complemented these efforts with local collaboration to support recruitment and implementation. This was less a new strategy than a matter of seizing opportunities. During rapid growth under Obey-Porter, SFA had been adopted district-wide in such high-profile districts as the Chancellor's District in New York City, Hartford, Lawrence, Columbus, and others. These concentrated adoptions created opportunities to extend the overall infrastructure by incorporating districts as members of the SFA network. SFA took the occasion to renew its work at the district level, especially by involving district staff in its Leadership Academy program. The academy was more an extension of the comprehensive school reform program than a brand-new district design, but it aimed to give the network greater reach into the proximal environments of schools and to improve the prospects for effective implementation.

In 2001/2, SFA began leveraging the improvement cycle to adapt to anticipated changes under NCLB. Chief among its efforts was to fashion a special version of Success for All called "Success for All—Reading First." In doing so, SFA targeted what it expected to be an expanding market for comprehensive school reform following the reauthorization. As explained in promotional material,

To align Success for All with the requirements of Reading First, we have created a new program, Success for All—Reading First, which is designed to meet these requirements. It builds on the programs, practices, and training capabilities established over the years by the nonprofit Success for All Foundation.

Success for All—Reading First is not merely an element of Success for All. Every aspect of the classroom program for grades K–3 has been examined in light of the Reading First guidelines and in light of changing state and national standards for practice and content. Many new elements are being introduced in Success for All—Reading First to strengthen the alignment with Reading First guidelines, and to improve professional development, assessment, curriculum, and other elements.[28]

Anticipating an emphasis on scientifically based research under NCLB, SFA secured funding to launch its most rigorous evaluation to date: a randomized study of SFA's effectiveness. The aim was to produce rigorous evidence of program effectiveness at precisely the moment that research-proven effectiveness was becoming a central focus of federal policy.

SFA: Reprise—the Implementation Puzzle

The results of SFA's early 2000s improvement cycle were remarkable. In four quick years, while continuing to support its installed base of schools, SFA appeared to have vastly increased its potential to support expert use through simultaneous, evolutionary improvements in its strategy for recruiting schools, its design, the organization, and its relationship with its environments. The Success for All enterprise also now appeared very strongly positioned in response to NCLB, two of its flagship programs (Comprehensive School Reform and Reading First), and its increased attention to scientifically based research in educational reform. At the same time, a new series of dysfunctional interactions among the schools, the design, the organization, and its environments had many schools still struggling to capitalize on that potential. And, very unexpectedly, these same interactions also had SFA struggling for survival.

Interactions—Design by Organizations

SFA's successes were matched by a new set of dysfunctional interactions, beginning with those between the improved design and SFA as an organization. To start, the amount and urgency of development activity between 1999 and 2003 overwhelmed historically informal means of coordinating work within SFA's development organization. Developers struggled to coordinate informally with each other, and lead developers, who were the hubs of improvement activity, struggled to stitch together SFA's many ongoing improvement efforts. What seemed from one perspective a strength—SFA's commitment to continuously improving the program—seemed from another to be a weakness. As Barbara Haxby, SFA's director of implementation, explained,

Success for All is a design that came out of a university, that came from people who do research. If that's where you're beginning your reform effort, research is rooted in collecting data and doing real field research and trying to figure out, "What are the issues that are out there, and does this program address it or not address it?" And some of that, I think, is historical, on where the model originated. There's a real strong culture. And that's both the good news and the bad news. The good news about that is we really pay a lot of attention to the field and to what we're seeing. The bad news about it is it does mean that you're always changing the program. It's so much more complex.[29]

Problems of coordination within the development organization led to problems of coherence in the design. Put plainly, many of Success for All's extensively revised program components were not tightly integrated so that they worked in mutually reinforcing ways, especially as a consequence of disconnects and redundancies between improvements to the leadership and instructional components. The early 2000s improvement cycle did include two efforts to address problems of integration: the Building Better Readers series (the school-based curriculum for teachers' professional learning) and the Goal-Focused Improvement Process (which integrated program improvements into a cyclical continuous improvement process). However, these initiatives came late in the improvement cycle, and partially in response to recognition of problems of integration in the program.

Uncoordinated development and weakly integrated design improvements created logistical and financial problems for the organization. SFA had to print, warehouse, and pay for the production of many new materials, though uncertain of the school-level demand for the new materials, and with urgent development activity quickly rendering recently printed program materials obsolete. Rapid obsolescence and unpredictable demand meant that SFA had to absorb much of that cost, which one executive estimated to be millions of dollars per year.

Further, urgent development and weakly integrated design improvements also created problems for SFA's training organization. The training organization had been strained entering the 1999–2003 improvement cycle, with its informal communities of training practice overwhelmed by the rapid recruitment of large numbers of inexperienced trainers while SFA struggled to develop formal systems to support their work and professional development. However, it was not until SFA began pressing the training organization to support a rapid succession of weakly integrated design improvements that it began to fully recognize and appreciate problems in the training organization. Indeed, it was only as trainers struggled to support the expert use of an even more complex design that SFA began urgent efforts to develop formal systems to support their work and learning. But by then SFA was deep into the early 2000s improvement cycle.

Interaction—Design by Organizations by Schools

Dysfunctional interactions between the design and SFA as an organization effected new problems in schools. These problems began with SFA's strategy for releasing program improvements to schools. Just as SFA did not formalize project management, it also did not formalize dissemination of design improvements to schools. Improvements were not packaged like software, as "SFA Version 2.0," but were sent out to the installed base of schools more like software bug fixes and repairs, improvement by improvement. Further, for SFA's voluntary paying customers, this process was driven largely by schools' decisions about which improvements to purchase, with different schools making different decisions about which design improvements to enact.

Consequently, between 1999 and 2004 a flood of weakly integrated program improvements rushed into Success for All schools, though differently for each school. Schools sampled new materials and training opportunities within tight budgets, sometimes based more on a component's curb appeal than on schools' needs. An unintended consequence was that the effort to improve the design and disseminate it to more than 1,500 schools re-created some of the very problems that SFA wanted to solve. One was faddism, as schools used scarce resources to adopt a mix of flashy and useful improvements. Another was "Christmas tree reform," as schools mixed and matched design components without careful attention to their integration. Another was distrust. For some schools, SFA's legitimacy rested on its commitment to continuous improvement. Yet, for others, the rapid flow of weakly coordinated design improvements had them questioning whether SFA had its act together.

All of the preceding further amplified the pressure on SFA's already struggling training organization. Weaknesses in integration and dissemination made an already complex design even more so, since there were so many more resources for schools to apprehend and use. Further, the improvements were to be used in SFA's large network of weak schools, requiring the "reform of the newly reformed." School staffs needed to unlearn much of what they had learned about SFA, and to learn that SFA was more than they suspected: not a bureaucratic tool but a challenging resource for professional practice and learning. However, doing so meant that trainers first had to manage the school-level integration of these many, rapidly disseminated program improvements.

The design revisions addressed real problems and made sense. But their dissemination and use compounded problems of coordination and capability, both in SFA's organization and in schools. The revisions also added to the burden on trainers, intensifying the stress on that already stressed part of the organization. Barbara Haxby, SFA's director of implementation, explained that continuous improvement while working at a large scale was considerably more difficult than continuous improvement while working at a small scale:

Not only are we doing a whole lot more stuff. There's just the communications piece across 1,600 schools and 250 different trainers, all of whom are remote. If you decide you're going to change something on Tuesday, it doesn't get changed Tuesday night. When there are five of you sitting around a table at Hopkins [early in SFA's work], you say, "Let's do it this way on Monday." And everybody says, "OK, I'll go out and do it that way on Monday." It's really different.[30]

Interactions—Design, Organizations, Schools, and Environments

These problems would have been difficult enough, but they were compounded by developments in environments. Following the reauthorization of ESEA as NCLB, the emergence of state standards and tests in all fifty states complicated efforts to adapt curricula in response, to develop information systems to reference and analyze state tests, and to help trainers (many of whom worked in several states) to adapt their work to changing state expectations. Further, deep into its 1999–2003 improvement cycle, economic turbulence as a consequence of the dot-com bust greatly reduced funding for education reform, including the philanthropy that fueled SFA's development organization. Once abundant support for design improvement was quickly growing scarce.

At the same time, as states, districts, and schools began to enact NCLB, the increase in scale anticipated by SFA's leaders failed to materialize. SFA executives soon recognized that schools were not enlisting in comprehensive school reform programs in general or in SFA in particu-

fessional development programs for trainers (long a source of weakness within SFA).

These efforts went further, to include the founding of three new organizations that would be managed by SFA executives and that would extend SFA's capabilities. In 2004/5, SFA cofounder Robert Slavin established the federally funded Center for Data Driven Reform in Education (CDDRE), which served as the context within which SFA developed the bulk of its leadership initiatives. In 2006/7, CDDRE and SFA's research operations were reorganized as a subunit within the newly founded, federally funded Center for Research and Reform in Education at Johns Hopkins University (CRRE). CRRE was also directed by Slavin, and it also collaborated with SFA in developing, supporting, and researching pre-K–8 reading programs. And, for 2007/8, Slavin was named director of the newly founded Institute for Effective Education (IEE) at the University of York in the United Kingdom. The SFA/IEE collaboration was yet another platform to advance the cause of research-validated programs. Further, it functioned as a potential source of revenue, in that it opened up potential for IEE to contract with SFA for its own development initiatives.

Environments

All of the preceding were matched with aggressive efforts to secure environmental conditions that would favor both continued success in the comprehensive school reform market and entry into the new, NCLB-affected markets. Some of these efforts extended strategies that SFA had been using since its inception: for example, publishing and publicizing what SFA executives saw as favorable outcomes of its national randomized field trial of SFA.[14]

At the same time, SFA began to pursue three new strategies. The first strategy, initiated in 2005, had SFA and other program providers requesting two federal investigations into the administration of the billion-dollar Reading First program. In 2006, the Department of Education's inspector general confirmed SFA's view. As detailed in the *Final Inspection Report*, the inspector general reported that the US Department of Education had:

Developed an application package that obscured the requirements of the statute; Took action with respect to the expert review panel process that was contrary to the balanced panel composition envisioned by Congress; Intervened to release an assessment review document without the permission of the entity that contracted for its development; Intervened to influence a State's selection of reading programs; and Intervened to influence reading programs being used by local educational agencies (LEAs) after the application process was completed. These actions demonstrate that the program officials failed to maintain a control environment that exemplifies management integrity and accountability.[15]

The inspector general later issued five additional reports that expanded on these findings, along with comprehensive recommendations for overhauling Reading First. Corroborating reports from the Government Accountability Office also revealed suspect practices in the government's university-based technical assistance centers.[16] While they provided no financial recourse, SFA executives viewed these findings as creating opportunities for more evenhanded treatment in state and district adoption processes. They also reported that the findings provided a morale boost for SFA staff members.

Riding the momentum of these favorable findings, the second strategy had SFA attempting to influence federal legislation by advocating for language, resources, and incentives to privilege research-based and research-validated programs: the Proven Programs for the Future of Education Act of 2007 and the Educational Research and Development to Improve Achievement Act of 2007. Much as the Obey-Porter CSRD Act of 1997 and the Reading Excellence Act had shaped NCLB, SFA executives hoped that these two acts would shape the forthcoming reauthorization of NCLB. As reported in *Education Week*,

Both bills say "research-proven" programs are those evaluated by at least two studies that use academically equivalent control and treatment groups, include sample sizes of five or more classes or 125-plus students, and use standardized assessments rather than developer-created measures, among other criteria. "The hope is that some of what's in these bills could get folded into NCLB," said Robert E. Slavin, a co-founder of the Success For All Foundation. . . . Mr. Slavin helped write the proposed definition in the Senate bills.[17]

The third strategy was familiar to both AC and AS Plus. Building on its experiences partnering with a small number of districts during its early 2000s development cycle, SFA sought to enlist districts and states as partners in recruiting and supporting school-level improvement. For districts, SFA used its Goal-Focused Improvement Process, web-based information system, and quarterly benchmark assessments as the basis for the "Data Driven District." This was a process model to be enacted jointly by districts, schools, and SFA trainers with two goals: evaluating

THE SUSTAINABILITY PUZZLE

school improvement needs, and selecting and implementing improvement programs shown by research to be both effective in improving student achievement and replicable across schools. The Data Driven District
model then served as a foundation for providing ad hoc assistance to
states.

To support this third strategy, SFA also collaborated with CDDRE to
establish the "Best Evidence Encyclopedia," an alternative to the federal
"What Works Clearinghouse." With that, SFA positioned itself as an arbiter of research-validated programs by conducting syntheses of available research and publishing its findings on the web. The goal was not
only to provide schools with evidence of the effectiveness of SFA's own
programs. It was also to create, identify, and privilege a critical mass of
providers committed to using research-proven programs. Like AC's and
NCEE's report on education and the economy, SFA's development and
promotion of the Best Evidence Encyclopedia could be interpreted as an
attempt to gain favor for such programs in an environment over which
it had no authority and little influence.

SFA: Reprise—the Implementation Puzzle

Between 2003 and 2008, SFA's multiple approaches to sustaining and
improving its enterprise appeared to pay off. After continued declines
through 2004/5, the installed base using SFA's comprehensive school
reform program stabilized at 1,200 schools for three successive years
(2005/6 through 2007/8), with an average time-in-program of over eight
years. Further, SFA's internal restructuring and cost-cutting measures
meant that it only needed to enlist sixty new schools per year in its comprehensive school program to remain viable. Finally, SFA executives reported a dramatic transformation in the performance of its schools, with
an estimated 75% advancing to some level of expert use and with only
an estimated 25% still mired in novice use.

SFA also succeeded in gaining entry into NCLB-affected markets for
school improvement services, thus creating new sources of revenue without having to develop extensive infrastructure to support implementation. By 2008, SFA reported that over 2,500 schools were using its new
targeted programs (primarily its quarterly benchmark assessments and
web-based information system). Further, in collaboration with CDDRE,
SFA reported that it was providing programs or services to 380 districts
and seven state education agencies. Capitalizing on this success, SFA was
also preparing to commercialize the Data Driven District model as the
"Raising the Bar" program, with responsibilities for development and

support moving from CDDRE to SFA. Finally, the combination of organizational streamlining and new revenues from targeted solutions had SFA operating in the black.

As with AC, SFA had succeeded in quickly transforming itself from a single organization that supported a comprehensive school reform program into a multiorganizational enterprise that supported a wide complement of programs and services in schools, districts, and states. Despite these successes, SFA's reprise of the design puzzle also reprised the implementation puzzle. And, again, new interactions among schools, designs, the organization, and environments created new questions about the effectiveness and sustainability of the enterprise.

Interactions—Schools and Design

As with AC, it simply was not clear whether less impacted schools, districts, and states would be able to use SFA's new programs and resources effectively. Paired with efforts to support implementation using self-study strategies rather than direct training, SFA's new targeted program closely resembled the nonsystemic solutions that SFA had long argued to be insufficient for effecting deep change in schools.

Complicating this concern was that many of SFA's new targeted programs were in the throes of formal evaluation during this period of rapid scale-up. Though SFA sought to become a champion, provider, arbiter, and broker of research-proven programs, the research base for the key elements of its entry into the NCLB-affected school improvement markets was thin compared to its comprehensive school reform program. The legitimacy of entry into the new market derived as much from its reputation as a provider of research-proven programs as from actual evidence of effectiveness.

Interactions—Schools, Design, and Organizations

Again as with AC, working urgently to support many new schools using a wide array of new programs created new pressure on SFA as an organization. Indeed, SFA developers reported that they sometimes felt like they were working at cross purposes. On the one hand, developers needed to better integrate SFA's comprehensive school reform program to address problems that had arisen during its prior improvement cycle. On the other hand, they also needed to unbundle the comprehensive school reform program to devise targeted programs for stronger schools, districts, and states. Developers needed to do all of this work more efficiently against tighter budget constraints while, at the same time, engaging in the messy, inefficient exploratory learning that is part and parcel of new program development. Developers needed to work patiently and with more coordination so as not to introduce new problems of integration and fragmentation into the program, yet they also had to work urgently to quickly gain entry into new markets. As SFA launched these many, simultaneous initiatives in 2004, one experienced developer spoke for many in the organization:

People are struggling right now, because we've changed so much in response to policy, the big changes being Success360 and the 4Sight Benchmark Assessments. Now we're going to offer these little components, and offer a kind of service that we haven't offered before and a kind of product marketing that we haven't offered before. And I think we're right at the transition point now where everyone sort of understands that we're doing these new things, but I don't think most people know what that means. And I feel like timelines are changing. Stuff needs to be done even faster, and promises are being made. And people are saying, "What's going on?" But I think they don't understand the pressure.

I almost feel like the organization needs to sit down and have a lesson in, "Here's what we need to start achieving for us to be competitive and to survive and to continue doing good things for kids. We need to start rolling stuff out this fast. We need to start developing this fast. We need to be this responsive in this kind of way." And I think the heads of departments know that, and the work is starting to get done by people in the departments. But people are feeling upset or flustered or they don't understand the reason behind what they're doing very much. And I think it's interesting. We're asking people to operate really differently. Suddenly, it's like we're sort of a publishing house.

. . . I feel like there's this bus, and it's going down the street. And we've missed it, and we're running to catch it. And we're not really sure where it's going, but we know we need to get on it. That's kind of what we feel like. "Oh, my God hurry! I don't know if it's going to go anywhere, but I think we're supposed to be on it!"[18]

Further complicating the stress on the organization was turbulence among SFA's executive staff. By 2006, the corporate leaders newly recruited to SFA had left the organization. By 2008, SFA appeared poised for its first executive transition. Due in no small part to political fallout following their push for the federal investigation of Reading First, SFA cofounders Robert Slavin and Nancy Madden were devoting more attention to the new Institute for Effective Education in the United Kingdom.

In their absence, they were delegating more responsibility for the day-to-day operations of SFA to less senior members of SFA's executive team, who lacked the founders' knowledge, experience, and connections.

Interactions—Schools, Design, Organizations, and Environments

Problems with schools, designs, and the organization were exacerbated by problems in SFA's environments, beginning with SFA's decision to develop relationships with districts and states in order to expand and sustain the enterprise. This strategy had the benefit of increasing scale, visibility, and especially revenues. At the same time, this strategy had potential to undermine the stability and sustainability of the enterprise, in that it left SFA vulnerable to precisely the same weaknesses and turbulence that AS Plus and AC had experienced earlier. For example, much of SFA's essential new revenue derived from partnerships with the state, districts, and schools in Pennsylvania, in good part through the use of SFA's new quarterly benchmark assessments and information system. One hiccup in Harrisburg—change in the governorship, the composition of the legislature, the secretary of education, or the state's economy—could have profound implications for SFA's bottom line.

The problems continued with SFA's efforts to develop the Best Evidence Encyclopedia. In doing so, SFA sought to fill a role (evaluating the effectiveness of improvement programs) that the federal government itself was trying to fill by developing the What Works Clearinghouse. That opened up questions about conflict of interest between the roles that SFA was trying to assume, first, as an independent arbiter of research-based and research-proven solutions and, second, as a provider of exactly such solutions. SFA took measures to ensure that reviews posted on the Best Evidence Encyclopedia were fair and impartial, both by commissioning independent reviewers and by publishing reviews in peer-reviewed journals. Even so, critics could argue that Best Evidence Encyclopedia was little more than a front for promoting SFA's programs.

The deepest problems, however, rested in broader political and economic environments. By the time that SFA had completed its mid-2000s improvement cycle, the very policies that had driven SFA to its new sustainability strategy had unraveled. By 2006, supplemental federal support for comprehensive school reform had been zeroed out of the federal budget, leaving schools still using comprehensive school reform programs to rely primarily on federal Title I funds for support. By 2008, the budget for Reading First (the program that had driven the market for district-determined, component-based school improvement solutions) had been cut by a third—ironically, primarily due to a loss in political support that followed the very investigation for which SFA had pushed so strongly. By 2009, funding for Reading First would be eliminated. At the same time, the scheduled reauthorization of NCLB in 2007 had become bound up in the 2008 presidential election, which was further bound up in the historic economic collapse of 2008.

As SFA wrapped up its mid-2000s improvement cycle, the only thing that was certain was uncertainty. SFA had succeeded in sustaining itself through 2008, and it appeared relevant, viable, and poised to begin a third decade. However, the prospect for long-term sustainability was very much an open question. Beyond uncertainty in the reauthorization of NCLB, the Chief State School Officers and the National Governors Association would soon mount the Common Core, an effort to build more coherence that would be centered in the states, not Washington. That effort would be launched concurrent with a federal economic stimulus package that included formidable funding for education reform.

While it was clear that the interactions and effects among all this activity would have potentially profound implications for SFA, it was not clear that sustainability strategies devised in NCLB-affected environments would buoy SFA amid the turbulence. If the Common Core did materialize and if NCLB changed in response, SFA would have to adapt its more diffuse and complex enterprise in response, and at the same time that states, districts, and schools interpreted and respond to these same dynamics.

Accelerated Schools

As it exited its 1999–2003 improvement cycle, the newly fashioned AS Plus faced circumstances remarkably similar to those of AC and SFA. Its redesign and reorganization efforts appeared to have AS Plus as strongly positioned as ever to use its comprehensive school reform program to empower many schools to support powerful learning for students. At the same time, efforts to improve the enterprise resulted in interactions among its schools, designs, organization, and environments that undermined both the technical effectiveness and the continued viability of AS Plus.

In some ways, AS Plus interpreted threats from NCLB-affected environments much as did AC and SFA. Executives in the AS Plus National Center recognized increasing district and state involvement in school-level improvement. With that, they recognized a waning market for comprehensive school reform programs as well as a growing market for more targeted solutions in higher-performing schools.

In other ways, AS Plus executives interpreted the environmental threats as more grave. Specifically, they recognized that the ideological mismatch between AS Plus and NCLB were more consequential than originally anticipated.

AS Plus held to its commitment to guide each school's community of practitioners to discover their own school-specific vision for powerful learning in classrooms, so that the discovery brought a new sense of ownership and belief in the school community's strengths. However, in contrast to school-determined improvement initiatives, AS Plus executives saw NCLB as embodying principles of top-down decision making and externally imposed, one-size-fits-all solutions. In contrast to powerful learning, they saw these solutions as seeking to effect rapid improvement by focusing narrowly on preparing students for standardized assessments. And in contrast to engaging teachers as active designers and problem solvers, they saw these solutions as "teacher proofing" instruction, narrowing the curriculum, and reducing schools' professional development time and opportunities. Indeed, in a 2007 interview, AS Plus executives estimated that 60% of AS Plus schools were implementing a program approved under NCLB's Reading First, while also noting that no approved Reading First program was congruent with the ideals of AS Plus.[19]

One problem, then, was that the fundamental conflict between AS Plus and NCLB challenged the sustainability of AS Plus by complicating efforts to recruit and retain schools. Another problem was that this conflict complicated the commitment and technical effectiveness of those schools that continued to participate in AS Plus. Indeed, these dynamics began to undermine the very things that AS Plus had just spent much hard work putting into place. For example, though AS Plus required an extensive time commitment from schools, and though AS Plus matched that commitment with eighteen days of on-site support, AS Plus staffers discovered that school-level efforts to respond to NCLB often left little time to engage AS Plus. As noted by AS Plus director Gene Chasin, even teachers that believed in the model felt pressure to keep their jobs and, thus, to make NCLB accountability their priority.

A good example of what's going on (in one district) is . . . they got a new superintendent this year and she's very traditional and very top-down. We have eight schools there that are really doing beautiful, all of them are doing incredibly well. And she hasn't taken the time to assess. She's coming in with that focus of the test scores and the testing game. Never mind that only one of those schools missed AYP; all the rest made AYP. And those folks are concerned for their jobs. First and foremost they're concerned for their jobs. . . . You've got staff in tears because they know that to do what they need to do to have job security means doing what's wrong for their kids.[20]

Thus, just as with AC and SFA, AS Plus executives reprised the design and implementation puzzles. The pattern of interpretation, action, and reaction bore remarkable resemblance to that of AC and SFA, with AS Plus seeking to maintain its comprehensive school reform program while also broadening its portfolio to include more targeted solutions. So, too, did the pattern of results, with AS Plus facing new uncertainty in its effectiveness and viability.

AS Plus: Reprise—the Design Puzzle

As with AC and SFA executives, early interpretations of dynamics in NCLB-affected markets for school improvement services drove AS Plus executives to reengage the design puzzle to ensure continued viability and to improve school-level effectiveness. And, as with AC and SFA, decisions to expand the scope of AS Plus beyond comprehensive school reform drove changes in its schools, designs, organizations, and environments.

Schools

AS Plus began with the very same decision as AC and SFA: that is, with the decision to continue to serve the population of schools that had historically adopted its comprehensive school reform program while, at the same time, reaching out to a new population of schools that sought more targeted solutions. Like AC and SFA, AS Plus shared the goal of leveraging this new population of schools both to open new revenue streams and to support many new students. However, unlike AC and SFA, AS Plus sought to use its collaboration with this new population of schools as a means of recruiting them to the comprehensive school reform program.

With both populations of schools, AS Plus executives decided to focus recruitment on schools willing and able to buffer themselves from NCLB. Even in NCLB-affected environments, the executives reasoned that there was a small subset of educators who agreed with the ideas underlying AS Plus and its comprehensive school reform program, and that district offices could find funds without difficulty if they wanted this approach. They emphasized that any new recruits to its comprehensive school reform program must be grounded in philosophical compatibility.

AS Plus executives recognized that this would greatly reduce the pool of schools from which to recruit. But, again, movement to AS Plus already had executives deciding to forgo large-scale operations in favor of high levels of implementation in schools. Their decision about recruiting in NCLB-affected environments simply strengthened that commitment. AS Plus executives were determined not to exceed the rate of growth at which quality could be maintained. Indeed, in a 2004 interview, an AS Plus executive reported that the National Center turned down up to 40% of applicants to its comprehensive school reform program due either to weak commitment to the core ideas or to logistical barriers to offering service.[21] With respect to an ideal size, AS Plus director Chasin described the organization as "fluid." He indicated as few as forty schools using its comprehensive school reform program would be acceptable, while 250 schools would be ideal.

Design

Decisions about adapting the base of schools were matched with decisions to adapt designs to improve effectiveness and to ensure sustainability. In order to reach schools and districts in NLCB-affected markets, AS Plus executives made precisely the same decision as AC and SFA executives: they unbundled the AS Plus comprehensive school reform program into more targeted programs, though with a continued focus on building cultural capabilities.

Unlike AC and SFA, the decision was not to embed AS Plus methods and principles into extensively elaborated, self-supporting materials. Rather, AS Plus executives decided that the new targeted programs would represent AS Plus methods and principles through training sessions and services. Heeding its own long-held tenet of building on strengths, Chasin saw this approach as leveraging the expertise AS Plus had acquired through years of work with schools.[22]

With that as the broad strategy, the new targeted AS Plus programs included management and instructional services for charter schools and what were often called "turnaround" schools. They included continued development of the AS Plus Leadership Academy (which focused on building distributed leadership teams in schools), as well as support for using AS Plus–provided tools to conduct an "Instructional Audit" that identified how well its instructional principles were being enacted. And they included one-day professional development seminars called "Accelerate Now" for full districts.

Again, AS Plus executives did not expect the unbundled programs to generate major change in schools. Rather, the goal was to use the new targeted programs as resources for recruiting more informed and committed schools into the AS Plus comprehensive school reform program. In contrast to a quick program adoption process, the new targeted programs were the basis for a long-term courtship that had potential to increase buy-in by increasing schools' knowledge of the central tenets of AS Plus.

Indeed, even with these new, targeted programs, and even in the face of a waning market, the core focus within AS Plus continued to be its comprehensive school reform program. AS Plus saw its comprehensive school reform programs as its core business and thus the primary focus of recruitment, program development, implementation support, and more. Schools would continue to be the key unit of improvement, and cultural and organizational change would continue to be central mechanisms of improvement, all toward building teachers' capacity to design and enact powerful learning in classrooms. AS Plus continued to see this approach not only as sensible but also as at odds with school improvement strategies that had emerged under NCLB. As AS Plus director Gene Chasin explained in 2008,

It's not about the programs you implement. It's more about building capacity around governance, curriculum, instruction, instructional delivery, decision-making, community engagement, and ultimately ownership in the school. . . . Typically when people reflect on their own practice they think it's pretty good, but when they reflect on their school they see big gaps. So typically what you see or what schools buy into, if you will, is the school moving together toward improvement and, as a unit, being able to use data to inform decisions, have the entire staff buy into and support those decisions actively. So you don't have isolated pockets of excellence. Rather, a whole school is moving toward excellence in a coherent way and building up the kind of community support that's necessary to fully implement an initiative. Particularly in the last eight years, decision-making has been by remote control in school communities, especially in schools that aren't performing well. They feel disengaged from the process of the schools. They feel like things are being done to those schools without them having any input, without them having any information about it.[23]

Given its centrality to the enterprise, AS Plus renamed and trademarked its comprehensive school reform program as "AS Plus Academies." From there, AS Plus extended improvement initiatives that it had begun during the 1999–2003 improvement cycle with the primary goal of supporting more high-quality implementation across a smaller base of more committed schools.

Though at odds with what the executives saw as the "quick fix" orientation driven by NCLB, AS Plus began by extending the initial contract with schools from three years to five years in order to create the time needed to support deep, school-driven change in culture, governance, and practice. From there, AS Plus continued to build school-level infrastructure to support implementation. For example, AS Plus continued to more clearly specify the program's goals and methods and to clarify connections between both cultural and instructional change in schools and classrooms. It revised its implementation benchmarks, implementation assessments, sample instructional strategies, and descriptions of the implementation process. As described above, it developed resources for an Instructional Audit used to evaluate and guide the use of culture to change instruction. It developed new training support, including a new Leadership Academy for principals and coaches, and web-based training for new teachers in experienced AS Plus schools. And it expanded the comprehensive school reform program beyond elementary schools into middle and high schools.

Organizations

The reorganization of AS Plus in 2003 had increased capabilities in the National Center for recruiting, program development, and marketing, as well as for iterative strategizing, planning, and adapting. Further, decisions made about schools and designs during its mid-2000s improvement cycle had potential to improve recruiting and revenues without increasing the demands on the organization to begin engaging in fundamentally new categories of work.

Even so, AS Plus leaders recognized that improving the prospects for technical effectiveness and long-term sustainability still required improving the leadership and capabilities of the National Center. An initial step was to create two new associate director positions within the National Center, one to increase capabilities for business management and policy analysis and the other to lead the continued development of the program.

As with AC and SFA, an even stronger next step was to make a fundamental change in the constitution of the National Center. Where AC reincorporated as a for-profit organization, and where SFA diversified its own organization by establishing an array of associated centers, AS Plus moved its operations into the newly established Institute for Urban School Improvement (IUSI) at the University of Connecticut's Neag

School of Education. Supported by state legislation and established in collaboration with an array of stakeholders in Connecticut, the goal of IUSI was to promote school improvement through local control and grassroots action.

Toward that end, the new IUSI incorporated three freestanding, ideologically consistent comprehensive school reform initiatives under one umbrella: AS Plus; Atlas Communities of Schools; and a new, Connecticut-specific initiative called CommPACT Schools. With the founding of IUSI, Gene Chasin left his position as director of AS Plus to head IUSI, and an experienced staff member assumed day-to-day responsibilities for AS Plus.

Membership in IUSI had the potential to benefit AS Plus in the short and long term. The alliance provided ideological reinforcement and collegial support for AS Plus as well as a morale boost for its staffers. Indeed, promotional literature describing CommPACT used ideas and language long used within AS Plus:

CommPACT offers a process for inculcating new norms and reinforcing existing (compatible) norms to provide a cultural foundation for the work of the schools. This foundation fosters development of highly effective learning environments in classrooms and a professional learning community among faculty. Cultural transformation and/or affirmation are especially important for schools in which challenges and obstacles related to poverty abound. It is the commitment and will among adults in the school that form the foundation for a systematic data-driven decision-making process that begins with belief in equity and culminates in evidence-based solutions. Adults' ownership, alignment, and building on strengths are crucial to realizing students' ownership for learning. With cultural transformation, each person in the school becomes part of the solution. Everyone becomes resourceful and focused. The centrality of inquiry toward the aim of equal opportunity for learning and growth transforms the way of looking at problems. It develops both instructional support elements and technical improvements based on the needs and strengths of each school.[24]

Membership in IUSI also added new organizational reinforcement for AS Plus at essentially no cost to the organization. For example, membership in IUSI created the opportunity to share professional resources for management, research, and academic work. It enabled AS Plus to create a full-time sales and marketing position. It enabled AS Plus to participate in business planning led by consultants with extensive experience in comprehensive school reform. It increased opportunities to work with Neag faculty. And it created opportunities to shift resources among the three participating programs in response to shifting demands and needs. As one AS Plus executive explained in a 2008 interview, "the beauty of what we have with the institute—if Atlas goes through a period where they're downsizing and CommPACT's scaling up, I can shift some staff over from Atlas to CommPACT or vice versa, or to Accelerated [Schools]."[25]

Environments

AS Plus continued long-standing efforts to manage the interactions between its enterprise and its environments. For example, AS Plus continued its attempts to cultivate environmental conditions supporting its school improvement initiatives. Chasin continued to visit Washington regularly to lobby for change in federal policy, which he described more as a matter of seeking support for the AS Plus philosophy than as seeking opportunity to expand the installed base of AS Plus schools. Further, AS Plus worked with schools to buffer itself from hostile environments, both by working with schools to maintain their commitment and by ensuring effective implementation. After all, in NCLB-affected environments, nothing created breathing room like results.

Over its mid-2000s improvement cycle, perhaps the strongest efforts of AS Plus to manage interactions with environments came with its membership in IUSI. Indeed, beyond having profound implications for the organization, the decision to relocate AS Plus within IUSI also had profound implications for its relationship with its environments. Specifically, the decision linked AS Plus to a state policy initiative in Connecticut that resembled the split-level approach that AS Plus founder Henry Levin had originally sought at its inception, with the environment providing moral and technical support for schools' self-determination. Within the broader (and hostile) context of NCLB, membership in IUSI had potential to provide state-level support for school improvement strategies long championed by AS Plus.

AS Plus: Reprise—the Implementation Puzzle

As it exited its mid-2000s improvement cycle, efforts within AS Plus to adapt its schools, designs, organization, and environments were showing signs of paying off. For example, AS Plus succeeded in recruiting schools to use its new targeted programs. By 2008, the majority of new AS Plus contracts were for Accelerate Now, its new one-day professional development seminars for full districts. AS Plus also succeeded in maintaining the installed base of schools using its comprehensive school reform program. In 2008, AS Plus reported having 140 schools using its comprehensive school reform, half of which were charter schools. The other half included schools in districts that had actively supported AS Plus as well as alternative schools. Further, AS Plus reported that the average time in program had climbed to over seven years by 2008. Finally, in a 2008 interview, one AS Plus executive also reported internal research showing that 90% of AS Plus schools that had been implementing its comprehensive school reform program for at least three years were meeting state-level criteria for adequate yearly progress.[26] While meeting AYP was not necessarily consistent with the internal goals of AS Plus, it was certainly important in NCLB-affected environments.

While AS Plus appear to be succeeding both in sustaining its operations and improving school-level implementation, efforts to adapt the enterprise in response to NCLB-affected environments also had the effect of reprising the implementation puzzle, as new interactions among schools, designs, the organization, and environment again raised questions about the long-term prospects for AS Plus, many very similar to those raised in the cases of AC and SFA.

Interactions—Schools and Design

Despite reports of increasing success with its comprehensive school reform program, AS Plus still faced the same question as AC and SFA: Could its new targeted programs be used effectively not only to recruit new schools but also to improve leadership, instruction, and student achievement in large numbers of schools? While not exactly the primary goal of its targeted programs, measurable improvement was still the coin of the realm in NCLB-affected environments. Yet AS Plus was working with the same sort of weak schools, in environments that were at least as difficult as before. Though AS Plus tried to build infrastructure that would offer more clarity and support for schools' work, it remained to be seen whether the new targeted programs could be used effectively, as well as what the consequences of either effective or ineffective use would be for AS Plus.

Interactions—Schools, Design, and Organizations

While its adaptations were enacted with the intent of minimizing the demands on the organization, inherent in the training-intensive approach of AS Plus was that doing anything at all in schools would place at least some strain on the organization. Indeed, both the new targeted programs and the revised comprehensive school reform program continued to emphasize a nonprescriptive, process-oriented approach to building professional capability that required extensive on-the-ground support, especially in weak schools operating in complex environments. Indeed, AS Plus staff members estimated that there was a day of preparation for every day of delivery.

More pressing for AS Plus, though, was uncertainty in its new organizational home, the Institute for Urban School Improvement. The history of US education reform is rife with the creation of centers and institutes of different types, advancing different solutions for different problems and populations. The leadership and lifespan of such centers and institutes is notoriously turbulent and linked tightly to turbulence in broader policy and funding patterns. While the IUSI had great potential to serve as both a refuge and stronghold for AS Plus, it also had great potential to disappear as quickly as it appeared, or for its mission to change dramatically with changes in policies, funding, and leadership. As AS Plus wrapped up its mid-2000s improvement cycle, neither the short-term nor the long-term prospects were clear.

Interactions—Schools, Design, Organizations, and Environments

As with AC and SFA, a final set of questions centered on the possible implications of uncertainty in federal financial support for school improvement. For AS Plus, the elimination of federal Reading First funding created uncertainty in the market for new targeted programs and services, and the elimination of federal supplemental support for comprehensive school reform created uncertainty in the market for its signature comprehensive school reform program. Indeed, from 2006 (when federal funding was eliminated) to 2008, the installed base of schools using the AS Plus comprehensive school reform program declined by over 40%, from 240 to 140. With that, AS Plus had reached a precariously small scale for a national effort. Where the bottom was in the waning market for comprehensive school reform programs simply wasn't clear.[27]

Thus, as AS Plus exited its mid-2000s improvement cycle, it did so with its usual precarious mix of promise and peril: successful and viable from one perspective, yet uncertain and vulnerable from another. This condition was exacerbated by uncertainty in the reauthorization of NCLB, in the 2008 presidential election, and in the broader economy (including the subsequent stimulus). In 2008, AS Plus director Gene Chasin was hopeful, regularly referring to the point at which "the [policy] pendulum swings back" to favor goals, values, and approaches to improvement consistent with those of AS Plus.[28] Yet, with the gathering Common Core standards movement, banking on enduring instability in the educational environments for a possible reprieve did not look like a promising strategy. More likely, AS Plus would need to continue steering the program through the same ideological headwind that had challenged it throughout its entire existence.

Conclusion

The three interventions undertook an extraordinarily ambitious task: that of improving America's weakest schools by building the educational infrastructure that most schools lacked. Yet achieving and sustaining success within their enterprises (i.e., their schools, designs, and organizations) depended on environments that created both major opportunities and major barriers.

The chief obstacle was that public education in the United States never developed the educational infrastructure that is common in the school systems of many developed nations. There was no common curriculum, no examinations tied to that curriculum, no system of teacher education grounded in that curriculum, and no means to prepare educators to manage teachers' and students' work within such a curriculum. Instead, each school or school system chose its own texts, and most left curriculum to teachers. Teacher education was grounded in no curriculum that teachers would use in schools, and schools used tests that were carefully designed to have no relation to any particular curriculum. The results, too often, were weak capabilities and incoherence both in environments and in schools.

If schools were to have substantial, coherent instructional programs, either their staffs had to devise some sort of infrastructure and sustain it through changes in people, policies, and local circumstances, or an external agency had to design and develop it and help schools to use it. Few schools or external agencies had done such work. It was unfamiliar. Few saw it as important. The work is very difficult. As our account in the preceding chapters shows, doing such work requires more than designing and implementing some sort of infrastructure; it also requires improving and sustaining it in the course of managing complex interactions among schools, designs, external organizations, and environments. Managing well requires knowledge, and that meant collecting and analyzing information on activity in and around schools. Doing that well required a large and sophisticated staff, and that required a good deal of professional education. These things and others were costly, and so another task was to raise the funds to sustain the operation. In an education sector in which legitimacy had long depended chiefly on complying with institutionalized expectations, few organizations had capabilities for such multifaceted expert work.

Not only were such capabilities rare; they were also unevenly distributed. Predictably, efforts to create infrastructure were less common in high-poverty schools, in part because schools in the United States are very unequal. Local and state revenue is the source of the funds with which schools hire teachers and purchase materials, and local and state revenues are very unequal. Schools in Mississippi spend less than half of what schools in New Jersey spend, on average, and the wealthiest local districts in New Jersey spend more than twice as much as the poorest districts. In many if not most other nations, schools are funded centrally, and students have more equal access to educational resources. The result for the United States has been that improved instructional programs were less familiar in the high-poverty schools that needed them most acutely.

The presence of such infrastructure and equal funding do not eliminate inequality or create excellent education. Those things depend on how well the infrastructure is designed and how effectively it and other resources are used. But more nearly equal resources, more common in other nations, would put schools on a more nearly equal footing as they tried to improve.

Hence, as they took on the task of improving many of America's weakest schools, the interveners took on problems central to US public education. Thus they had to do a great deal of work that, in a reasonable world, would have been routinely done by established agencies: teacher education that focused on curriculum that was used in schools and would support ambitious learning; social services that would deal with students' health and nutrition problems; educational resources that were more equally distributed, and so on. The interveners could not even count on a pool of expert teachers, teacher educators, and school leaders from which they could draw to staff schools and their organizations. They either had to create that pool with their own professional education or search for expert needles in educational haystacks. These circumstances placed significant limits on their work: they could succeed only in part because so many underlying problems—poverty, poor health, educational inequality, and more—were beyond their reach.

These circumstances also led the interveners to devise infrastructure and help schools to use it. Their efforts to do so were entirely sensible, given the situation and their desire to improve education, but the effort had enormous costs. Not only did the interveners have to invent or adapt assessments, curricula, teacher education, and school management; they also had to find or devise ways to help educators to understand it and learn to use it well.

AS Plus dealt with these and other problems by delegating most of the work of finding or devising instructional infrastructure to the schools with which it worked. Yet those schools operated in environments that offered little assistance with and many impediments to improvement. Our colleagues' research found that students' learning in ASP schools was no better than that of otherwise similar students in schools that had no intervention.[29]

SFA and AC's invention and adaptation of infrastructure was a large part of the reason that they achieved some success, but they had to build organizations that could do the work, which was demanding, costly, and required continuous revision in light of schools' use of the designs. That greatly complicated their efforts, requiring them to build large and complex organizations, to find and educate more staff, and to raise more money. Hence, as we wrote earlier, the better they did, the more difficult it became.

Despite their different strategies, the three organizations faced two common problems. One was that the more they sought to do in more varied types of schools, the more the interventions depended on organizations in the environment for money, recruits, and expertise. That made them more vulnerable to changes in the environment, a problem that became vivid with the advent of NCLB.

There was no way around this entanglement. The interveners could not have achieved their successes had it not been for their environments. The New American Schools (NAS) initiative made it legitimate to devise and field comprehensive school reform programs, and it put money behind the work in the late 1980s and early 1990s. State and federal standards-based reforms pressed schools to improve and created demand for the intervention designs. The 1997 Obey-Porter Comprehensive School Reform Demonstration Act enhanced the legitimacy of such work and boosted demand for the interventions' designs with grants to states that enabled them to support schools that adopted them. That created a market for the services of SFA, AC, and AS Plus, among others. It also enabled the interveners to develop their designs, schools to adopt their designs, and to achieve their remarkable scale. Never before had there been such an intense effort to devise and implement systemic solutions to the problems of high-poverty schools, and it was produced by remarkable actions by NAS, the interventions, and federal and state policies and managers.

Yet these fruitful developments meant that AS Plus, AC, and SFA depended on the environment that NAS, Obey-Porter, and standards-based reform created for mission, funds, legitimacy, schools, knowledge, and expertise. If things had remained stable, the interveners would not have faced the new uncertainty that we discussed in this chapter, nor the consequent threats to their sustainability. They could have continued with their prior mission, niche market, customers, and funds, focusing primarily on engaging the challenge of improving the technical effectiveness of their enterprises.

But environments did not remain stable. The interventions' early 2000s improvement cycle was marked by the dot-com bust, 9/11, and NCLB. These sudden shocks were not followed by comparative calm, and their effects rumbled and ramified through the nation during the entire first decade of the new millennium, straight through the interveners' mid-2000s improvement cycle. Even though the mid-2000s showed signs of economic recovery, a historic economic collapse followed that dwarfed the dot-com bust. Economic turbulence was tied in no small measure to two wars abroad and a changed policy environment in which education competed with more urgent concerns for public and political attention as well as funds. Throughout those years, the management of NCLB was continuously negotiated and renegotiated by federal, state, and local education agencies.

The result was new—and, for the interveners, difficult—dynamics in school improvement. As written and administered, NCLB created strong incentives for state and local education agencies themselves to move more aggressively into school improvement across the full complement of schools, both weak and strong, yet it did not offer them much assistance to build the capability to do the work. Hence, state and local agencies began to compete with AS Plus, AC, and SFA while, at the same time, becoming potential clients for the school improvement capabilities that the interveners offered. NCLB also put growing pressure on local districts to improve their weakest schools, something for which few districts had the capability, and that fed continuing demand for the whole-school designs that had made the interveners' reputations.

Through all of these changes, two things remained stable. One was pressure for improvement from standards-based reform. Another was funding for school-wide improvement under Title I of the federal Elementary and Secondary Education Act. Both worked to the advantage of AS Plus, AC, and SFA, for they created demand for their programs and services and money to support their adoption.

This combination of deep turbulence and modest stability created incentives for the interventions to improve and adapt in ways that played to their strengths. They developed new designs to appeal to new clients and to accommodate change in the market for school improvement, which led to change in their missions. All three retained their comprehensive school reform programs as the core of their operations, but they also created programs, products, and services that either drew on portions of those designs or moved in quite different directions. These changes led to change in the three organizations' constitutions: AC became a for-profit organization, SFA became a constellation of nonprofits and centers, and AS Plus was incorporated into a new nonprofit center. AC maintained the size of its central organization, but AS Plus and SFA downsized: the former as part of an intentional strategy of exchanging quantity of schools for quality of implementation, and the latter as part of a response to difficulties recruiting and retaining schools in turbulent environments.

The other problem that the three faced in common was that they were private sector agencies, situated outside the public school system, that were trying to change schools and build quasi-independent systems inside the public sector. This offered them some advantages, including the independence needed to develop a mission and purpose around complex and novel solutions and then organize to pursue that mission and purpose. It is very unlikely that their work ever would have been done by public sector agencies, let alone by the public schools. Hence, their position outside the public system was crucial.

Yet, in order to do their work, they had to be deeply entangled in that public system. They intensified the problem by choosing to work with schools that were part of that system, rather than working close to its boundary in new charter schools. For the interveners, this meant that they depended on the public system for access to schools and for the legitimacy that the system could confer by selecting them, by evaluating their work, and by funding them. Much of their money came from that public system through Title I funds. In good times and bad, they depended for these essential resources on the system that they were trying to reform. For the schools, this entanglement meant that every member of every school in the interveners' networks was also a member of the system of public education. They were committed to the interventions that were trying to change public education, and they were committed to the education system that was being changed. The two very different systems overlapped almost entirely, and collided not only in the schools but also in the ideas and loyalties of those at work in them. As the schools and interveners invented and managed their own systems, those systems embodied the paradoxical relation with the environment of which we write.

In 2008, as we closed our study, AS Plus, AC, and SFA seemed stable—at least for that moment. Yet they faced daunting problems. Nobody knows what the Common Core, the Obama administration's Race to the Top program, or the reauthorization of NCLB will mean for these three enterprises, never mind the most dire economic turbulence since the Great Depression. Will these developments interact in ways that stabilize the environment of education and provide opportunities for AS Plus, AC, and SFA to work more effectively? Will they destabilize that environment and impede the interveners' work? Independent of this environmental activity, what other options might the interveners pursue in addressing the sustainability puzzle?

SIX

Building Systems

The three interventions' most distinctive contribution was to build educational systems. They aimed to improve students' learning by making instruction more engaging and coherent, and they did so by working systemically. They rebuilt schools' culture to assure that they were animated by the same purpose—more engaging and effective teaching and learning—and they revised management and organization to support that purpose. They also provided the educational tools to achieve that purpose, including curriculum to guide instruction, professional education to help school staffs change practice, materials to support both activities, and much more. In these ways and others, the three organizations built educational infrastructure.

Their approach was unprecedented, for very few initiatives had ever made such a comprehensive effort to rebuild high-poverty schools. Most earlier school improvement schemes centered either on organizational change with no instructional content, like decentralization or mayoral control, or on efforts to change a single element of instruction, usually curriculum, thus dealing with a single part of instruction in isolation from the other parts on which it depended for effective use.

Our analysis in the preceding chapters has stressed two essential points: that the interveners' approach was unusually promising and effective because it took on fundamental weaknesses of US public education, but that the more seriously they took on those weaknesses the more problems they encountered. Every success that the interveners achieved brought them face to face with new puzzles. Most striking was that these puzzles were remarkably similar, despite formidable differences in the interveners' approaches. Their efforts to build educational systems and manage the associated puzzles improved schooling for many thousands of children, but their efforts also illuminated the problems and possibilities of the large-scale educational reform that federal and state policies have promoted for several decades, and which they promote today.

The latest manifestation of such reform—the Common Core State Standards Initiative (CCSSI)—is very likely to produce many of the same problems the interveners faced. We take up a few of the most fundamental issues here, because we think that understanding them could be useful to those who are interested in the CCSSI.

Systemic Improvement?

One persistent problem that the interveners faced was building infrastructure to change practice in schools. Few school systems in the United States had coherent educational instruments and the know-how to use them. To build such infrastructure and use it to improve students' learning, the interveners had either to invent new instruments and put them into coherent relations with each other, or to find them in the environment and try to assure that they would work coherently with each other. These things would have been difficult in any school system, but they were especially difficult because they cut against the deepest grain of education in the United States. This system had been structured to promote local control, the separation of powers, and weak government, and so core functions like testing and curriculum were outsourced to private firms. That impeded coherent action within and among schools and school systems.

Moreover, even if the infrastructure were built, teaching and learning might not improve, for new educational tools would only be effective if they were used well. That would depend on how clear and accessible the tools were, how committed school staff were and whether they spent time and effort to understand the tools, worked hard to make them function in practice, had ample opportunities to learn, and had sustained support.

But if sustained support was something that the interveners and schools needed, the conditions that we just sketched limited the capability of federal, state, and local agencies to provide it. State and federal agencies had few staffers with expertise in curriculum, learning, teaching, and teacher education. States had delegated most instructional decisions to localities, and most localities delegated them to schools. Many schools delegated them to teachers, as long as they maintained order in their classes. Most local school systems and the state agencies that govern education lacked the capability to create and support the elements of a common system of education, let alone to improve schools and systems.

Federal policies in Bill Clinton's and George W. Bush's presidencies sought to create the missing coherence, but they did so by requiring standards, tests, and accountability—things that operated on schools and school systems from the outside. There was very little attention to creating the capability inside schools that would enable them to make the changes that these policies urged. There was no support for common curricula, and most tests were not linked to any curriculum. Instead of a common academic structure and tools with which to improve work in schools, there were many different and often conflicting purposes, programs, policies, textbooks, and tests. Even the quality of teacher education varied. The political environment pressed schools to improve, and it created a market for the interveners' programs, but the new federal policies sought to create educational coherence in an environment that was quite incoherent, and to build common academic purposes in an environment that cultivated many different purposes.

The interveners could influence some of these conditions, but teachers' contracts, schools' policies, practices, and organization, and state and federal policy also influenced them, often constraining the interveners' abilities to improve conditions in schools. Peter Hill, then AC's director of research, pointed to one part of this problem in a 2002 interview:

When I first arrived, one of our first tasks was to try and get a more precise understanding of the effects we were having on kids' learning. And I'm from Australia, so I just said "Fine. Let's look at the assessments, and then we'll see where on the curriculum kids are not performing, and then we can look at how our design is working with different pieces of the curriculum." Because that's just the way it works in Australia. The assessments and the curriculum are tied together. And when I learned that the assessments here couldn't provide any information on the curriculum, I was very angry. I remember saying, "This doesn't make sense. We're not going to be able to learn anything."[1]

Such incoherent features of the environment were at odds with key elements of interventions. That made it difficult for people who worked in schools to take the new programs seriously, to understand them, to put them into practice, and to sustain them.

In order to deal with such incoherence and protect their work inside schools, the interveners sought to establish environments of their own.

They wanted to create coordinated, coherent relationships that enabled communication among schools, and between schools and the national centers and regional training organizations that they established. These national centers and regional organizations were vehicles for building a common culture as well as professional knowledge and skill, and they were staffed by educators who were trained to do such work. These organizations were also professional communities, whose members were tied together by common norms, common purposes, common methods, and common language. They were professional education agencies that helped teachers and school leaders learn how to turn the designs into practice. They were quality control agencies, collecting evidence about school staffs' practices and solving problems with the designs in schools.

But this work was neither easy nor inexpensive, and so another problem developed here. The interventions created counterenvironments to buffer their networks from the larger incoherence and to cultivate the education that they sought to promote. To do these things, however, they had to hire, train, and pay people to maintain the professional communities and their work, raise funds to support that work, promote communication among schools, buffer schools from problems in the environment, and advocate for their work in government and elsewhere. These things helped to inform, support, and protect work in schools, but they made huge demands on the interventions staff while also requiring huge resources in terms of energy, money, and time.

A third problem was that if school staffs were to effectively use the resources that the interveners offered, they would have to focus intensely on improving their practices of learning, teaching, and leadership. If the school systems had had the capability, they could have used the interveners' tools to change practice, but most school staffs lacked those capabilities. So it fell to SFA, AS Plus, and AC to do the intensive, close, and sustained work on practice that the schools needed. AC and SFA did that by paying very close attention to and offering strong guidance for curriculum, teaching, learning, and their organization in classrooms and schools. These interveners worked closely with teachers and students over many years to create instructional practices that were set out or implied in the designs, and they worked with school leaders to create practices of professional education, instructional management, and school leadership.

Yet the interveners did not enter the scene prepared to do these things. Instead, they had to create practices for their own staff to use with people in schools, in professional education, instructional management, and school leadership. They did not have the luxury to adopt or adapt tried-and-true practices, or to use existing research on how such work was best done to guide their work. They had to invent several sorts of practice as they went ahead with the work. By far the largest part of that work was design and development. Research contributed to this effort, but this was not a case in which innovators moved research to practice. Rather, it was one in which innovators used research as they worked with professionals to design, create, teach, and learn better professional practice and organization. They also used evaluations to investigate the effects of their designs and to legitimate them. This was not classical rational problem solving, which moves from problem diagnosis to research to new knowledge to practice, but a combination of design, development, and implementation, concurrent and interacting, often followed by re-design, redevelopment, and more implementation, also concurrent and interacting.

The task was practical and fast moving—improve high-poverty schools—so the interveners responded practically and dynamically. With accumulating experience and reflection, all three interveners learned that their costly and difficult focus on practice was fruitful but still inadequate. What they needed was a more comprehensive focus on practice, with equal attention to novice, intermediate, and expert practitioners. That included practitioners in schools. It also included practitioners in their own organizations: developers, trainers, researchers, and even executives.

Such work could not be done from a great distance, nor could it be done quickly. One reason that AC and SFA schools improved more than AS Plus's was that SFA and AC invested much more in the staff and organization to support schools' work. And one reason that state and local school systems have been unable to make much progress in school improvement is that they had little of the infrastructure that the interveners developed. It may seem ironic, but these interveners, who operated on the fringes of long-established public school systems, had more educational capability than most state and local school systems.

Successes Beget Challenges

Two decades of operation brought a paradoxical result: The better that SFA, AS Plus, and AC did in compensating for weakness and problems in schools and their environments, the more difficult their assignment grew. One reason for that result was the school reform policy environment. The Obey-Porter legislation, in an effort to support comprehensive school reform, flooded states with funds in a way that enlisted many uncommitted schools, led to too-rapid growth for AS Plus and SFA, and helped to create problems. A few years later, NCLB changed the frame in which the interveners and schools had to operate; among other things, it created new markets for school improvement to which the interveners tried to respond in order to survive.

Another reason for the paradoxical result was the problems that came with greater scale. As their reputations spread and policy pressure for improvement grew, the networks added schools. As they learned from early experience, their designs grew more complex, with more elaboration and more professional education. That led the interveners to hire more staff, to spend more time and money, and to grow more complex. AS Plus resisted the pressures through the 1990s and the first years of the new century, but then reduced the scale of its network and tried to boost its capability. In contrast, SFA and AC tried to maintain their scale while their organizations grew larger and more complex.

These changes required more coordination, management, and resources, and they took more time. Achieving the interveners' aims would have taken time in the best circumstances, but these were not the best circumstances. There were many environmental obstacles. School staffs had to unlearn a great deal. The designs, practices, and organization that enabled change had to be developed in situ in real time. Learning and change had to occur at many levels—classrooms, schools, networks, and central organizations—more or less simultaneously. When we began this study, the interveners thought that their designs were comprehensive, but they learned that the meaning of comprehensive is relative to the nature of the problem; to the complexity of instruction and schools; and to the sheer number of functions in classes, schools, environments, and organizations that required reengineering. The more they responded to problems in the schools and the environment, the more comprehensive their work became.

That affected the extent to which the schools could improve as well as the time it took. At the beginning, the interveners expected that schools could make significant improvements in three to five years. They assumed that the work would succeed if, when they stopped working directly with a set of schools, those schools would continue to perform at a high level. Things didn't turn out that way. The interveners did things that few public school systems even tried to do, and that the environ-

ment tended to impede: They built infrastructure among schools to connect them to sources of knowledge, to create communities of practice
and purpose, to share experience, and to buffer schools from the larger
environment.[2] However, those functions were not assumed by school
systems or other agencies in the environment, so schools were not likely
to sustain improved performance if the interventions left schools on their
own in weak school systems and environments. But if the interventions'
organizations were essential to sustaining schools' gains, membership in
the networks would be more permanent than temporary, and that would
limit the number of new schools an intervener could support.

One way to summarize these explanations for the paradoxical effects
of the interveners' success is that every school that joined one of the three
networks led a double life. Each belonged to a new professional community that stood outside the public schools, but each also belonged to
a public system. That double life was crucial for the interveners, because
they needed the schools' Title I grants, among other public and philanthropic contributions to schools, to fund the work. But the schools' double life also complicated the interveners' work, because the schools often
had rapid turnover of teachers, managers, and students, many poorly
educated teachers, weak and inconsistent leadership, and rapid change
in leaders and policy.

Hence, the interveners also led double lives. They needed the public
systems' participation and money, but they were at odds with those systems in fundamental ways. The interveners were trying to build purpose-
driven schools in public systems that had long avoided clear purposes,
because many were so controversial politically and difficult educationally. They were trying to build coherent schools in the midst of an enterprise that was deeply incoherent. Because the interveners took schools
as they were yet tried to turn them into something that they never had
been, they could only work by engaging the school systems and becoming vulnerable to all their weaknesses. They built school systems to do
what the public systems had not done, in the interstices of those systems,
while they depended on them for funds and political support.

Learning

One other dimension of the interveners' double lives concerns their connections with standards-based school reform. The three organizations
owed a great deal to these state and federal policies, for without their pressure for better education, there would have been much less demand for

school improvement and thus for the interveners' designs and services. But what the three organizations owed to the policies arose as much from what the policies could not do as from what they could.

Much of what we learned resides in that mixed legacy. The strengths of these policies were at the same time weaknesses, yet those weaknesses created hugely important opportunities for the interveners. Those who now are engaged with the Common Core are almost certain to face a version of this situation.

Standards-based reform sought to improve schools by using common standards of academic content, common tests of how well students learned the content, professional accountability for students' learning, and support for school improvement. These policies were constructive in several respects. They highlighted the importance of academic engagement and coherence in schooling and inspired many efforts to create more of both. Those were remarkable steps forward in political and educational systems designed to impede coherence and that often had deliberately avoided academically ambitious work with most students. The reforms also brought much more attention to inequality in public education at a time when America's attention had been elsewhere. And they shone a bright light on weakness in the quality of US schools, especially for students from poor families, and made it visible for politics and policy.

These were significant accomplishments, but they came with very substantial limitations. One was the view that weak schools would repair themselves with guidance from standards and tests, incentives from accountability, and some help with improvement from state or local authorities. But that view greatly overestimated the capability of most high-poverty schools. It overestimated what they could do on their own in response to standards, tests, and accountability. And it overestimated the state and local capability to help with school improvement.[3]

Another limitation was that standards and tests did not translate into common purposes, common professional norms, common curricula, and a common language for diagnosing and solving educational problems, nor did they turn into common practices of teaching, learning, and instructional leadership. We learned that standards and assessments could be useful elements of an educational infrastructure, but they are very far from practice, and they have been a weak guide to improved practice. Standards-based reform did little to support creation of expertise that would support teaching and learning, partly owing to political constraints on policy design and partly to overestimates of the policies' capacity to shape practice.

But the policies did offer incentives for schools to improve, and thereby created a market for the interveners' work. What was lacking in the policies were things that the interveners could invent and offer—that is, systems to create and sustain better schools for children from poor families.

From study of what the interveners did offer, we learned that educational infrastructure—curriculum, designs for teaching and leadership, and professional education—was key to substantial improvement in teaching and learning. We learned that building stronger practice in weak schools requires intensive work that is sustained for years. We learned that it is important to build educational infrastructure among schools as well as within them, so that improving schools can work within educational systems that support and protect them. All three organizations did these things, but AC and SFA did much more to build educational practice and content into that infrastructure, while AS Plus left it mostly to schools.[4]

We also learned that though the interventions took individual schools as the primary unit of intervention, theirs was never a scheme to reform one school at a time. In contrast to earlier efforts like "effective schools" and school restructuring, they saw that good work in individual schools would be more likely to prosper and endure if the schools were part of a system that protected and encouraged the work. As they built programs to support work in schools, they also built support at district, regional, or national levels to support and protect that work in larger systems.

In these ways and others, one of the interveners' greatest contributions was to enable members of our study team and other Americans to learn things that we had never seen because they had never been attempted in the United States. SFA and AC built educational systems that introduced something new and important: carefully crafted and well-specified designs for school improvement that could help schools to improve teaching and learning, and do so consistently at scale. They significantly improved teaching and learning in many of America's weakest schools. The interveners made visible the elements of system building that sustained improvement: educational infrastructure, coordinated relationships, and an intense focus on practice.

We began this book by discussing a dilemma: "Policy makers and others can define problems and devise solutions, but only the people and organizations that are the problem can solve them, perhaps with help from others."[5] After all, organizations such as AC, ASP, and SFA could no more "improve" schools than teachers could "learn" students. The interveners showed that they could manage the dilemma; they were able to help schools with serious problems to devise solutions. The three were among a small group of comprehensive school reform providers that had some degree of success in terms of scale, sustainability, and effects on student achievement. The others include Direct Instruction, Core Knowledge, First Things First, the Literacy Collaborative, the National Writing Project, the School Development Program, School Renaissance, and the Talent Development High School model.[6]

Yet AC and SFA did not succeed as much as they had hoped, and AS Plus did not discernibly improve instruction in the schools that we studied.[7] Their success was limited partly because the dilemma holds for people and agencies in the environment, as well as for those in schools. For in order to help schools to improve, the interveners had to cope with inadequate teacher education, weak school district management, an incoherent array of educational programs, and policy churn, among other things. Many problems that manifested in schools arose in the environment, so the interveners tried either to turn the environment in a constructive direction or to compensate for its weakness. But that meant that the more they tried to solve school problems, the more the interveners tried to solve environmental problems. The better they did, the more difficult their work became.

The problems and opportunities that the three interveners encountered are likely to be endemic to any effort to use policy instruments like standards and assessments, which operate on schools from the outside, to change operations inside weak schools operating in the fragmented, hyperactive environment of US educational politics. The Common Core is the latest invention of that sort, and it has many potentially promising features. But for reasons that combine limits on the political influence of state and federal governments with limits on their educational capability, the Common Core has attended much more to standards, tests, and some guidance for curriculum than it has to building capability to use those standards, tests, and curriculum effectively. Despite its potential strengths, the Common Core has not attended to a central problem: how will it design and support direct work with schools to improve teaching and learning? Instead the new initiative continues past efforts to improve schools indirectly, with more focused standards and tests, opening more charter schools, or recruiting more able teachers.

Those measures could help. More able teachers certainly would help, and more focused standards and better assessments could. But if these and other Common Core initiatives do help, it will be because some agencies help schools turn them into fruitful practices for teaching, learning, and school leadership. Two sorts of organizations do such work: a small number of comprehensive school reform providers (SFA, AC, AS Plus, and the others identified above) and a small number of charter management organizations (with Aspire, IDEA, Achievement First, and KIPP as leading examples).

These organizations will be crucial to the new reforms, because they develop the knowledge, know-how, and other capabilities that will be required if the reforms are to work and endure at any scale. One sort of knowledge concerns what it takes to make an "effective school"—that is, the know-how of effective teaching and leadership, and the practices that can support the development of that know-how in schools. Recent reforms don't deal with such matters, yet our research shows that delegating the creation and use of such crucial knowledge and skill to weak schools, as federal and state policies have done, is not a recipe for success.

Another sort of know-how concerns turning ineffective into effective schools, commonly referred to as school turnaround. This is work in which AC and SFA have extensive experience, and that a few charter management organizations are now starting to do. Most other school turnaround efforts have failed most of the time. The best recent estimates are that turnaround, in schools and other organizations, succeeds in one of every four or five cases.[8] It is difficult to understand why federal policy makers have ignored the expertise of AC, SFA, and other similar comprehensive school reform providers as they try to encourage and support school turnaround.

Still another sort of knowledge concerns the systems that support and sustain school improvement—the networks that support good work in individual schools and classrooms, and the know-how needed to build and sustain these systems. It includes recruiting and educating staff that can help to teach teachers how to improve students' reading, building organizations that support and protect schools as they improve, knowledge of how to sustain such enterprises in turbulent environments, and more.

And yet another sort of knowledge concerns the nature of different strategies for large-scale, network-based school improvement. SFA and AC led with strong and detailed guidance for teaching, organization, and management; AS Plus led with change in schools' values and culture. We expect that there are other strategies, and thus more to be learned from studying how interveners pursue and combine them in efforts to improve large numbers of schools. Description and analysis of such strategies could benefit efforts to support schools' response to the Common Core. In addition, though we expect that future interveners will face puzzles that mirror what we reported about SFA, AC, and AS Plus, that conjecture merits evaluation. Perhaps the problems of school improvement vary more dramatically with the strategies that improvers adopt than we expect.

These few paragraphs refer to an unusual combination of facts, understanding, practice, and dispositions that support comprehensive and large-scale school improvement. It is scarce in the United States, especially in high-poverty schools, yet it is essential to the improvement of high-poverty schools. Most of it is not written down. It resides in the interveners and their networks, in individual people and their work, in groups, reports, materials, structures, norms, relationships, and routines. The interveners' unusual position on the border between research and practice, combined with their systematic efforts to collect and analyze data, made them unique generators of and repositories for knowledge of comprehensive, large-scale school improvement. Unlike most school systems, these organizations are deeply immersed in the day-to-day life of schools. For example, they regularly collect and use evidence from hundreds of schools. Unlike most textbook and test publishers, they regularly examine the relationship between their programs, varied local contexts, student populations, and learning outcomes. Unlike most schools and departments of education, they structure teacher education around learning how to teach particular subjects to particular students in particular sorts of schools, rather than learning about teaching in general. Though the chasm between research and practice is often wide and deep in education, initiatives like AC and SFA generate a brand of knowledge that arises in practical efforts to improve schools, and to use theory, research, and professional experience to that end.[9] They aim not to show "what works," but to learn how particular resources work in local contexts to improve particular students' learning.

Knowledge of this sort has been sorely lacking, yet the success of the Common Core is likely to depend on whether means can be found to generate and use it.[10] We have no idea whether agencies associated with this initiative will try to create such organizations, and we are not inclined to adventure in a crystal ball. But we have learned a few things from studying school improvement that illuminate what sorts of organizations could do the job, and what it might take to create and sustain them.

There presently are two sorts of suitable organizations: some version of the comprehensive school reform providers that we discussed here, and a few charter networks that seem to be developing the expertise to manage educationally effective systems of new schools. The creation of many more organizations of either sort would require several steps. One would be a detailed description of possible designs and an analysis their strengths and weaknesses, the likely time required for start-up, and the cost of operations and staffing requirements. Another would be government and private money to support the improvement of existing designs with proven effectiveness, and still another would be support for the invention of promising new designs.

More crucial to the ongoing work of school improvement would be funds to maintain networks to support improving schools, and state legislation to authorize franchises of proven designs, so that staff in the existing comprehensive school reform networks who already have the required expertise could create new hub organizations and networks of improving schools. It would be wise to define such networks so that they operated within a single state or large district, or groups of small states; that would protect them from the huge logistical problems of operating national systems. State legislation also might be required to enable charter networks that satisfied the requirements for designs and operation akin to those of comprehensive school reform programs.

There is no large pool of skilled workers ready to take on such difficult work in challenging contexts, and they would be needed. So it also would help if those networks (or other agencies that worked closely with them) could offer high-quality professional education for teachers and school leaders who would work in high-poverty schools. The idea would be to offer professional education that was grounded in and focused on the specific practices and ideas that define the schools and network in which teachers would work. It would have to be authorized by state governments and supported by state, federal, and private organizations. Very few institutions of higher education have ever tried to offer such education, and few seem prepared to undertake such work, even now.

It is unlikely that these things could be done wholesale. For some time to come, improvement would be piecemeal. That is sad, but the efforts of charter networks and comprehensive school reform providers require intensive work on a relatively small scale, in schools and classrooms; it cannot be done effectively in huge systems. That is one reason we favor franchising some proven comprehensive school reform programs. What is more, educators, policy makers, and philanthropists have a great deal to learn if the work is to be done well, so it should be staged in ways that encourage rather than defeat learning. National or state programs that are required to demonstrate success on fixed schedules would impede learning. That has been a central weakness of NCLB, for its wholesale approach, tied to compliance schedules and requirements of statewide and national success, led quite predictably to defining down the criteria of success, as well as to inhibiting the trials and errors that are an unavoidable element in any serious learning.

At the same time, the benefits of piecemeal improvement would depend on whether there would be systematic learning from the work. Hence it would be important to create or adapt agencies that could organize continuing efforts to learn from practice improvement, and equally important to encourage school improvers and others to use what would be learned. These things would require agencies that monitor and improve the quality of teaching and management, which requires close observation and consultation, incentives to use the advice, and support for schools to use it. It would be a mistake to tightly tie rewards and punishments for schools to the results of such studies, for that would create strong incentives to politicize the reporting and distort criteria of quality, as occurred with NCLB and many local and state reforms.

This is not what Americans regard as "accountability," but it could not work without serious commitment to educators' responsibility for quality. One example of agencies that encourage such responsibility in other nations is inspectorates, in which staff members visit schools and classrooms, assess the quality of work, offer reports and advice, and help with improvement. Another example, in the interveners that we studied, is field staff that did some of that work, as did school-based coaches and facilitators. There is anecdotal evidence of similar work in a few of the charter networks. When such agencies are useful, it is because they combine experienced judgment, institutional memory, and close familiarity with practice in relationships that are designed and situated to improve teaching and management. Building cohorts of people who can do this work would take time, money, and expertise.

We have no idea whether such things will be done, in part because we see rather mixed signals. On the more encouraging side are several promising recent initiatives. One is the federal Investing in Innovation (i3), which continues to support school improvement networks pursuing improvement by design. Another is a research program proposed by the Institute of Education Sciences to support continuous improvement in school systems. Still another is an effort by leading philanthropies to develop "communities of practice" among the leaders of these large-scale, system-building efforts; the funders include the William T. Grant Foundation, the Spencer Foundation, and the Hewlett Foundation.

Less encouraging is the very well established structure of state and federal education policy, familiar from the Clinton and Bush administrations. Because these policies focused on academic standards, tests, accountability, and charter schools, they did not attend to directly improving teaching and leadership practice in schools. Yet few schools or school districts can do it themselves, nor can state or federal agencies provide the required guidance and assistance, for most lack the capability. It also is work that cannot be done from a great distance or at a great scale, whatever the agency. Despite these considerations, the Obama administration's policies also seem to assume that practice in schools and classrooms can be changed by policies that press schools from the outside without also rebuilding them from within.

One thing that we are sure of is that both school-level and larger educational infrastructures are necessary to substantial and sustained school improvement. Common curricula, curriculum frameworks, and common and coordinated assessments could be very useful, but they are not likely to help very much without organizations like SFA, AS Plus, and AC that can build the within-school infrastructure and practices and mobilize the people that can make them work. That is unlikely to occur at any scale unless those who make policy recognize that only sustained, close work in schools and classrooms can turn the educational tide, and create the means to encourage and support that work. Such measures would be consistent with the current federal and state drive for greater coherence in education, but they would need to move well beyond current policies. For it is only close work on learning, teaching, and leadership that can bring standards, curricula, and assessments to life in schools.

Appendix:
Research Procedures

This research was part of the Study of Instructional Improvement (SII). Researchers at the University of Michigan School of Education, in cooperation with the Consortium for Policy Research in Education (CPRE), conducted a large, mixed method, longitudinal study of the design, implementation, and effects of the three most widely adopted whole-school reform programs in the United States: the Accelerated Schools Project (ASP), America's Choice (AC), and Success for All (SFA). Each of the three sought to make comprehensive changes in schools, and each was implemented in high-poverty elementary schools, yet each pursued a different design for instructional improvement, and each developed its own strategy to assist schools. SII selected the three because they represented rather different approaches to school improvement, which promised illuminating comparisons.

SII devised a program of research to examine how the three intervening organizations operated, the effects of their programs on teaching and learning in reading and mathematics, and how they influenced school leadership and organization. There were three main research components, which were intended to complement each other.

- A longitudinal study of teaching and learning in 115 schools (roughly thirty schools in each of the three whole-school designs under study, plus twenty-six matched control schools), using a variety of survey research methods.

- A longitudinal case study of three sets of three schools (one set per intervention), plus three matched control schools that used none of the interventions.
- A longitudinal study of the three interventions that focused on the ideas that guided them, the implementation strategies the staffs devised, how they were organized, and their work with schools.

Though SII undertook the three studies as an integrated research program that examined instructional improvement from several perspectives, each study planned to issue its own reports. All three examined the designs for instructional improvement, the strategies for putting the designs into practice, and the extent to which the varied designs and strategies promoted changes in instructional capacity. Only the first study also investigated student achievement in reading and mathematics. A list of project publications is available at www.sii.soe.umich.edu/about/pubs .html.

This book draws from the third of the three SII components. This third component began with an effort to understand the interveners' designs for school improvement and the ideas behind them. Since a design is no more than a design until it is used, we also investigated how the designs fared in practice and how the interveners changed the designs in response to the schools' efforts to put them into practice. We investigated how the interveners organized to carry out and support their work with schools as the scale of operations changed. Finally, we sought to understand interactions among the designs, the schools using them, the intervening organizations, and the environments within which the enterprises operated, for it was in those interactions that knowledge for instructional improvement was created. The study's longitudinal design was essential to all of this. We extended our work to more than ten years, well past its planned end, and that was a key "method." We learned as the interventions developed, and the designs, the scale of operations, the environment and organizations changed.

David K. Cohen was the principal investigator, Karen Gates was the lead analyst for the Accelerated Schools Project, Joshua Glazer was the lead analyst for America's Choice, and Donald J. Peurach was the lead analyst for Success for All. Ruben Carriedo, Matthew Janger, James Taylor, and Christopher Weiss were early members before moving on to other positions. Simona Goldin joined our group in 2002. Team members assisted in instrument development for the other two components of SII.

In what follows, we present an orderly summary account of our data collection and analysis, in an effort to make clear what we did. Yet as most researchers will know, though we carefully planned for orderly work, the reality was more spontaneous, emergent, and sometimes puzzling than our plans. For example, though we discuss analysis and data collection separately below, analysis began with data collection, and the two developed in tandem. The relationship between them was more dialectical than sequential, and more fruitful for that. We regret the retrospective reification of experience, but were we to represent things as they actually occurred, we would have had to spend nearly as much time documenting our research procedures as we spent doing the research, and we then would have had to write a book portraying our research procedures. We did not have the time or chutzpah for the first, and we doubted that readers would have had time or patience for the second.

Preliminary Work

SII began in 1996 with initial investigations, sampling of designs, instrument development, and researcher training. The work of our group began with a seminar that ran from 1996 to 1998 which analyzed materials from several comprehensive school reform programs, including Core Knowledge, School as Community, and Outward Bound, as well as SFA, AC, and ASP. This work and conversations with the designers led to the selection of the three interventions on which we report in this book. Responsibility for continued preliminary research fell to several different members of our group. Their exploratory work focused primarily on the designs' "theories of action," designs for school restructuring, and their evolution as organizations. By 1999, we had assembled considerable data, including a complete library of program materials; internal articles, research, and reports; external evaluations and critiques; field notes from visits to schools; notes and analyses from interviews with school teachers and leaders; and notes and analyses from meetings with intervention executives and staff members.

Between January and August of 2000 we completed three comprehensive, hundred-plus-page technical reports, each of which summarized all data collected to that point on SFA, AC, or ASP. We devised six analytic categories that captured key issues across programs: theory of intervention; instructional design; support for implementation; school recruitment; scale-up; and design, management, and improvement of the intervening organization. We identified twenty-seven subcategories within these six, and used them to structure our initial analyses.

Data Collection

When we turned to study the interventions in operation we used participant-observation, interviews, document collection, some video, and informal conversation. Because the intervention organizations and methods of operation varied—for example, ASP was a much more lean organization with many fewer staffers—there were some differences in the frequency of interviews and observations among the interventions.

Participant-Observation

Beginning in 2000, we used participant-observation to deepen our understanding of the designs, organizations, and schools. One aim was to learn about the designs just as people in schools learned about them, and another was to gain access to knowledge not captured in program materials. Joshua Glazer, Karen Gates, and Donald Peurach took on the roles of school trainee and researcher, but with emphasis on the latter. Sometimes this involved listening to presentations, or working with small groups, or examining student work samples, or analyzing video of classroom instruction. It was not always possible to remain detached in these events, for small groups quickly broke down social barriers, and our comments were sometimes solicited. Such participation may violate some views of methodology, but our understanding and field notes were richer for it. To immerse oneself in the work of people struggling to learn new practices, to develop the persona of an "instructional leader," and to muster the courage to admit one's own insecurities and doubts is to learn that any given design is not simply a collection of processes and practices. For those who must enact a given design and take responsibility for others' enactment, a design is a frame for what can be a difficult and sometimes transformative experience. We hope that some of the flavor of this experience has found its way into our account.

Regarding SFA, Donald Peurach's participant-observations ran from May 2000 to January 2010, for a total of thirty one-to-six-day training events spread over seventy-three contact days. In these training events, Peurach assumed the role of the intended learner (e.g., teacher, school leader, or SFA trainer), and he engaged all contexts and tasks exactly as the intended learners did. In school years 2000/1 and 2001/2, Peurach attended all training for new schools using SFA's reading and mathematics programs, once per month Leadership Academy sessions (which included observing implementation in eight schools), and the annual

Experienced Sites Conferences. From 2002/3 through 2009/10, Peurach attended annual Experienced Sites Conferences: up to 2007/8, as a primary venue for data collection, and thereafter to maintain observation of SFA while completing our analysis. At two points (June 2002 and June 2004), he repeated the week-long initial training for school leaders. In addition to attending training for schools, he was a participant-observer in four training events for Success for All trainers in 2001, 2002, and 2008, for an additional seven contact days. For all training events, he compiled handwritten notes and event-specific materials into a single field note that included purpose; background information; room layout; descriptions of trainers and participants; materials; chronology of activities; content covered; and notes and observations as they related to our analytic categories, as expressed in informal conversations, as related to observations made in other sessions, and as emergent.

Regarding AC, Joshua Glazer observed eleven training sessions for principals and coaches from November 1998 until April 2004. Topics included reading, writing, math, school leadership and training for AC staff. Trainings were typically full four-to-five-day events. Glazer selected sessions to attend based on multiple criteria, such as the topic to be covered (e.g., use of a newly developed set of materials), the facilitating staff member, corresponding events in the environment (e.g., change in federal legislation), or events in the AC organization (e.g., turnover of key staff). He took detailed field notes for all training sessions and wrote a summary analysis of each. On four occasions, he accompanied AC staff on school visits during which they evaluated implementation and worked with school leaders to solve problems. These schools were selected for purely practical reasons, such as an America's Choice staff member issuing an invitation to attend or an impromptu event that offered an opportunity to visit a school. These visits enabled Glazer to learn how AC field staff viewed implementation and to observe some of the things that influenced schools' capacity to interpret and use the design. On four occasions he attended NCEE's National Conference, which brought staff from AC schools from around the country to discuss a broad array of issues related to design and implementation, to hear guest lecturers, and participate in workshops. These conferences provided an opportunity to learn about changes in the design, including the development and release of new materials, as well as chances to speak with field staff about their work.

Regarding ASP, the decentralization of development and training responsibilities led Karen Gates to design her participant-observation to investigate constancy and variation in the training, assistance, and school design across ASP satellites. Two complementary strands of observation covered the years before and after the introduction of AS Plus (see chap. 5 for a discussion of the change). Each year she also observed all national events, including conferences for school practitioners and events specifically for principals and other school leaders. She also observed satellite-specific training in nine of eleven satellites, including events for new and continuing schools and covering ASP's full array of training topics. With the reorganization to AS Plus, she observed sites that remained affiliated with the national center and continued with one satellite that did not affiliate. Altogether, Gates observed forty-seven multiday training and assistance events, eleven of which were national or regional. Three included classroom observation within schools considered high implementing, each in a different region.

Interviews

As our understandings and interpretations developed, we began to talk with intervention staff about issues that had developed in our preliminary research and observations. We held more than one hundred formal interviews, either in person or on the telephone, but we had thousands of informal conversations with teachers, leaders, and staff members over more than ten years of data collection. These conversations offered opportunities to learn about the use of the programs and the work of school improvement, and to discuss ongoing analyses and interpretation. For example, most training events were designed to create social opportunities for participants from schools and staff members from the intervening organizations, and training sessions were designed to encourage social interaction and collaboration among participants. We kept notes and observations from these conversations and pursued them further in document analysis, training events, and formal interviews.

Regarding SFA, Donald Peurach conducted three groups of semistructured interviews with program executives, developers, trainers, researchers, and operations staff. For the first group (which ran from 2003 to 2005), he conducted sixty-two interviews with twenty-two people who represented a range of roles, responsibilities, and experiences. The interviews were designed to investigate how this large improvement program was launched and sustained. For the second group (which ran from 2005 to 2006), he interviewed four people who had left SFA, to understand the conditions of their departure and capture reflections on their experience. For the third group (which ran from 2005 to 2008), Peurach conducted eleven interviews with SFA executives to discuss how SFA was sustained amid the turbulence that followed NCLB's passage. Peurach took handwritten notes during all interviews, and thirty-six of the seventy-seven interviews were recorded and transcribed. The remaining interviews were not recorded either at the participants' request or due to the sensitive nature of the topic under discussion. He wrote reflective memos following each interview to capture emerging themes and key observations. After completing a wave of interviews in a given year, he wrote a summary report of interviews for the year.

Regarding AC, Joshua Glazer conducted thirty-three formal interviews between 1998 and 2010. Interview subjects included the executive leadership of NCEE and AC; the directors of field operations; lead designers in reading and writing; upper-level staff and chief program developers; and field-level staff (including cluster leaders and regional directors). At the upper level of the organization, he interviewed the same individuals on multiple occasions. The selection of field staff was determined by several considerations including their experience with and knowledge of America's Choice, their specific responsibilities, and their involvement in particular regions where the design was being implemented. Most, though not all, interviews were audiotaped and transcribed. For those that were not, notes were written immediately following the conversation. Prior to an interview, Glazer designated key topics of conversation, focusing on the design of the intervention, the overall improvement strategy, problems with implementation, and possible changes in future strategy.

Regarding ASP, its lean central organization meant that the count of interview subjects was lower than for the other two interventions, for a total of eight formal interviews with executives from ASP's National Center and its leading satellites. The interviews dealt with the same themes, including what did and didn't vary across geography and over time. All interviews were audiotaped and transcribed. Formal interviews were supplemented by hundreds of conversations in person or by phone, including national events attended by leaders from all satellites.

Documents

From the beginning of the study, we collected all the paper and electronic documents we could find in an effort to track the design and operation of the interventions.

Regarding SFA, Donald Peurach compiled a library of documents and artifacts concurrent with his participant-observation and interviewing. The library includes three editions of the SFA-published trade book detailing the origins of the program, the design components, sample curriculum materials, and research on Success for All: *Every Child, Every School* (published in 1996), *One Million Children* (2001), and *Two Million Children* (2009). The library includes five editions of the primary leadership manual (1996, 2000, 2002, 2004, and 2006), which lays out the whole program for internal use. And the library includes the primary manuals and associated materials for instructional and supplemental components at three intervals (1996, 2000, and 2004); collections of participant training books from Success for All training events that mark the evolution of the program over time; annual conference brochures and materials catalogs, which also mark the evolution of the program; and many other materials (e.g., videos, CDs, DVDs, forms, trainers' materials, promotional literature, research reports, media accounts, and government documents).

Regarding AC, Joshua Glazer collected three sets of primary sources. An initial source of information came from two funding proposals. Though such proposals often present a sunny view of an organization and its prospects, they also provide useful snapshots of how leaders view the work and goals of the organization as well as their intentions and assumptions. A second set of materials included chapters and books authored by AC executives. These were written several years after the proposals and offered evidence of changes in thinking, lessons learned from experience, and changes in the environment. A third set of materials included curriculum materials and videos that AC produced for teachers and school leaders, as well as material designed for school leaders and for in-school professional development. These included the New Standards performance standards, which defined instructional goals for the first few years of the program, as well as the reference exams that measured progress toward those goals. All of these offered evidence of details of the design and intended classroom and leadership practices. Because they changed over time, these materials also offered evidence of change in AC's strategy.

Regarding ASP, Karen Gates collected three sets of documents. First, the national center provided SII with a full series of newsletters as of ASP's late 1980s founding, plus an extensive internal *Taking Stock Report* (1995) prepared by the national center and a 1999 conference paper authored by national center staff regarding the intervention's organizational structure. These materials also helped to clarify ASP's initial organizational strategies and challenges. Second, she collected material that ASP made available to schools, both nationally and within satellites, to advance understanding and use of the design. Primary national examples were the "Accelerated Schools Resource Guide"; two ASP-authored books intended to support implementation; newsletters from the national center; extensive website material prepared for schools; implementation benchmarks; and an implementation assessment instrument that was revised several times over the course of our study. At every training event that she observed, Gates collected the materials provided to trainees, nearly all of which were satellite-generated. Third, she collected third-party studies of schools' use of the ASP design and internal and external scholarly papers that addressed school design, organizational operations, managing the environment, and more.

The result was a small mountain of data that was not easy to organize and manage. In preparing the preliminary reports in 2000, we tried to use qualitative analysis software. Though the software was serviceable with small amounts of data, we soon stopped using it. The volume of data, the rate at which we collected it, and its many different formats complicated use of the software, as did differences in Windows and Macintosh computing platforms, changes in operating systems over time, and changes in the software. Instead we kept all hard copy and physical materials in chronological files and kept all digital documents in computer files: "Field Notes," "Interview Transcripts," "External Research," etc. We analyzed these data by pulling and printing documents, stacking and restacking, cutting-and-pasting, and marking pages and passages with Post-It notes and highlighters.

Analysis

We began this work in early 2000 with a provisional set of analytic categories and a summary report based on the preliminary data. As we continued into formal data collection, we initiated a process that would extend into 2010 and that would become our primary analytic procedure. Either weekly or occasionally biweekly, we produced three individual memos (one per program) in which we sorted newly collected and existing data into analytic categories. The categories changed somewhat as our understanding deepened, and we tested them against the evidence from each of the interventions. We did this by framing the memos with the analytic categories and trying to use them to inform the accounts of each intervention. We described this to ourselves as "writing into" our analytic categories, but it was also a continuing test of the utility of those categories. From two to four times a month for nearly a decade, we met to engage in within-case and cross-case analyses by comparing these program-specific memos, reviewing interpretations, pressing each other to push harder on the data, adjusting our categories, and identifying needs for additional data.

Our work together also was informed by work that several of us were doing separately. Don Peurach and Josh Glazer did their own analyses of SFA and AC respectively, initially for their dissertations and then to produce a stand-alone book (in the case of SFA) and to compare key issues at the intersection of AC and SFA. Peurach's independent research yielded what he described as a "functional framework" describing the core tasks performed routinely by SFA: designing programs; supporting implementation; scaling up the network and the organization; continuously improving; and sustaining the enterprise. His dissertation research also yielded what he described as a "contingency framework" that had schools, the program, and broader environments interacting in positive and negative ways to complicate the work of SFA as an organization. This became the chief analytic framework detailed in his book on SFA, and it was one forebear of the analytic framework used by the broader team.[1]

Joshua Glazer's dissertation portrayed AC as an attempt to develop a professional system of instruction. That built on the work of Andrew Abbott, offered a fresh view of professionalism as a system for organizing expert work in varied contexts, and focused on the tension between standardizing professional work with a set of routines as against basing practice on individual practitioners' discretion.[2] In discussing that tension, he examined how the internal architecture of the three interventions created varying knowledge demands on teachers, and how those demands affected the organizations. It led Glazer to speculate that one reason SFA's network was twice the size of AC's was that AC's design placed greater knowledge demands on teachers, in part because it required them to do much of the design work performed by SFA developers. That, in turn, required more professional education, staff, and training, and it appeared to limit the total number of schools with which AC could work.

As our work progressed, David K. Cohen and Susan L. Moffitt were doing the research for and writing a book on the relations between policy and practice in the case of Title I of the 1965 Elementary and Secondary Education Act (ESEA).[3] This program sought to use federal monies to improve teaching and learning for poor students in the United States, and it was an external intervention in many of America's least favored schools. In both respects, it resembled the three interventions that we studied. Cohen and Moffitt's analysis highlighted the influence that weak capability had on implementation, as well as the problem of weak educational infrastructure. Both ideas seeped into our work on this book.

Our work also was shaped by problems that followed from the decision to study the interventions and their supporting organizations. One problem was that the staff members in ASP, AC, and SFA saw things from the perspective of their own experiences with their own designs. Hence, those who worked for each intervening organization had a perspective that limited their view of the issues in our study, and for each of the three we could expect to hear their side of story. We dealt with this as we would have dealt with any situation in which the collection of any sort of data depended on respondents' knowledge and beliefs: We sought a variety of views on the issues that we investigated from sources within and outside each intervention.

Another aspect of this problem was our effort to combine sympathetic understanding with dispassionate or even critical analyses. We sought to do what some researchers might describe as "going native": that is, to understand the interveners and their interventions on *their* terms, to get as close to their understanding of their ambitions and designs for schools as we could, and to get as close to their view of their work in schools as we could. Initially we did these things to help with other components of SII: specifically, to inform the development of survey instruments, field protocols, and interview protocols, as well as to train other SII researchers in the complexities of the designs. As our work evolved, though, we wanted access to the motives, ambitions, ideas, and actions of the people involved.

But we also sought a dispassionate or even critical perspective. We wanted to understand the interventions from the outside as well as the inside, precisely because there are limits to any insider view of any set of events and great value in independent views of those events. We initially tried to do this by rotating analysts among interventions, but that was very costly in time and consistency of coverage. As our analyses unfolded, we incorporated outside perspectives by pressing each other for evidence supporting key claims, by offering and evaluating alternative explanations, by reviewed alternative explanations with intervention staff, by having two members of our team who were not tied to any intervention and who had not worked "inside" any of the three, and by drawing on other studies of school reform efforts.

In the end, we found that it was no easier to be sympathetic than to be critical. Colleges of education—at least those with no anthropologists—rarely teach methods of sympathetic analysis; they teach methods of dispassionate or critical analysis. Our efforts to be simultaneously sympathetic and dispassionate stretched us, for we tried to take two different roles and cultivate two different viewpoints on the same events, ideas, plans and problems, often at the same time.

One other continuing problem was what sometimes seemed to be a choice between narrative and analysis. The development and implementation of each design was a compelling story in its own right, for each had features that reflected unique elements of an effort to improve America's least favored schools. Yet all three were part of a common effort, and they shared many features. Moreover, several key analytic points were common to the three designs, and several others depended on comparisons among them. We wanted to tell the individual stories because so much of what it took to do the work was in those individual histories, but we wanted to discuss them together because there was such leverage in the comparisons.

This problem of analysis bled over into a problem of presentation: Would we write the book by leading with the analytic categories, or would we lead with the separate intervention histories? What would be the figure and what the ground? We wrestled with this on and off for years, as detailed in our discussion of the book's structure in chapter 1. As we wrestled with the structure, we began to understand that what was most important in our analysis was *not* the stories of the individual interventions themselves but, instead, the *common problems and challenges* that they experienced despite formidable differences in their approaches to improvement by design.

As such, we decided to structure the chapters as a sequence of common puzzles that unfolded roughly chronologically in the experience of the interveners; to structure the primary sections intervention by intervention in order to provide coherent accounts of each; and to use common subsections to structure comparisons across interventions. This puzzles-oriented structure bears close resemblance to the functionally oriented structured use by Don Peurach in his stand-alone account of Success for All. A key outcome of this analytically focused narrative was the chronological sequencing of analyses, which enabled us to compare across programs to identify and address overlaps and gaps in data and analysis.

These are among the distinguishing features of this study. We found no other account that offers a historical analysis of such complex interveners and interventions as they unfolded over time, in an analytic framework that is grounded not in their individual identities but instead in their common experiences.

Validity

Our data collection and analysis incorporated several efforts to establish validity which we alluded to above. We engaged in extended observation of the phenomena under study. We searched for opportunities to investigate "negative cases" that did not square with emerging categories and themes. We triangulated among different categories of evidence (i.e., field notes, interviews, and documents or artifacts). We critically analyzed each others' work and sought such comments from colleagues. We triangulated among our analyses of Success for All, America's Choice, and the Accelerated Schools Project. And we checked our evidence and interpretations, formally and informally, with intervention leaders and staff members.

From time to time we also checked our work with those who worked on the other two components of SII, with particular attention to confirming reports of intervention staff members regarding patterns of implementation, effects, and program improvement. We presented conference papers and defended dissertations, which opened up additional critical commentary. We solicited comments from ASP, AC, and SFA executives on our draft work, conference papers, and dissertations. We interviewed elected officials, researchers, and critics. We engaged in extended forays into the literature to deepen our understandings of key phenomena under investigation. And we critically read, reread, and revised our written analyses more times than we would care to count.

ASP had two concerns about validity. First, in response to early publications reporting on ASP's implementation and effects, ASP executives expressed the concern that the SII survey sample was skewed to low-implementing schools, and that their design had changed since the data was collected. On other occasions a senior staff member worried that ASP's process-based model did not fit well with SII's research.

One way that SII addressed ASP's first concern was to conduct special analyses of data. For example, Brian Rowan, SII's principal investigator for the survey component, presented analyses regarding variation in implementation, which showed that this did not affect the findings at issue. Lead researchers from SII's school case studies and survey component also prepared analyses regarding the elements of implementation in which ASP schools had stood out positively (e.g., cultural measures), in line with the design's emphasis. Our research group agreed to point out that ASP's design had changed since the time of the survey research (as had the other two).

In another effort to explore validity, we invited the leaders of the three intervening organizations to a day-long meeting in Ann Arbor, Michigan, in the late fall of 2006. We presented summaries of our findings and interpretations and listened carefully to their responses, both to our findings and interpretations and to each others' views. It was a fascinating exchange of ideas, and we learned a great deal about how they saw their own efforts, what they thought of our draft analyses, and how they saw each other's designs.

At that meeting we also had an opportunity to check whether ASP did fit into the study. We presented an essay with essential findings to start the discussion with all three intervention groups; the essay reflected our emphasis on a single analytic frame, and the features that all three shared. Each set of intervention leaders presented accounts of their work, including challenges and learnings. Their agreement with our view supported the validity of our understanding of ASP's fit in the study.

Karen Gates also prepared a written description of our view of the ASP design and its theory of action, and presented it to AS Plus leaders in a group interview in order to test our interpretation. We included their responses in the preceding chapters.

In the course of this study, we learned a great deal about the design and implementation of complex designs for improving teaching and learning, but we also learned about how to study such things. In chapter 1, we wrote that improvement efforts of this sort occur at the intersection of design, schools' capabilities, politics, finance, policy, and more. This meant that we would have to understand much more than the interveners' designs. Doing such work always requires time and patience, but in this case it also required the willingness to follow paths that often led well beyond the original research design.

If we had to write one sentence about what we did, we might say that we observed the interconnectedness of it all. That is not exactly a method of research, but it does capture the most important element of this study.

Notes

CHAPTER ONE

1. Throughout, we will refer to the programs for change in schools as "interventions" and "programs." Alternatively, we will refer to the teams developing and fielding those programs as "organizations" and "interveners."
2. National Center for the Accelerated Schools Project, *Taking Stock Report, Accelerated School Project* (internal document, 1995), xi.
3. This problem is discussed in more detail in David K. Cohen and Susan L. Moffitt, *The Ordeal of Equality* (Cambridge, MA: Harvard University Press, 2009), chap. 2.
4. See, e.g., Donald Boyd, Hamilton Lankford, Susanna Loeb, and James Wyckoff, "Explaining the Short Careers of High-Achieving Teachers in Schools with Low-Performing Students," *American Economic Review* 95 (2005): 166–71; Donald Boyd, Hamilton Lankford, Susanna Loeb, and James Wyckoff, "The Draw of Home: How Teachers' Preferences for Proximity Disadvantage Urban Schools," *Journal of Policy Analysis and Management* 24 (2005): 113–32; and Hamilton Lankford, Susanna Loeb, and James Wyckoff, "Teacher Sorting and the Plight of Urban Schools: A Descriptive Analysis," *Educational Evaluation and Policy Analysis* 24 (2002): 37–62.
5. See, e.g., Arthur Levine, *Educating School Leaders* (Washington, DC: Education Schools Project, 2005).
6. These two paragraphs are adapted from Cohen and Moffitt, *Ordeal of Equality*, chap. 1.
7. Amy M. Hightower, *District Bureaucracy Supports Culture of Learning* (Center for the Study of Teaching and Policy: University of Washington, 2002).

8. Success for All Experienced Site Conference, April 10, 2001. Field notes by Donald J. Peurach.

9. See, e.g., Boyd, Lankford, Loeb, and Wyckoff, "Explaining Short Careers"; Boyd, Lankford, Loeb, and Wyckoff, "The Draw of Home"; and Lankford, Loeb, and Wyckoff, "Teacher Sorting."

10. For one case in point, consider the Man: A Course of Study (MACOS) curriculum as discussed in Peter B. Dow, *Schoolhouse Politics: Lessons from the Sputnik Era* (Cambridge, MA: Harvard University Press, 1991).

11. Ibid.

12. David K. Cohen and James P. Spillane, "Policy and Practice: The Relations between Governance and Instruction," in *Designing Coherent Education Policy: Improving the System*, ed. Susan H. Fuhrman (San Francisco: Jossey-Bass, 1993).

13. Arthur G. Powell, Eleanor Farrar, and David K. Cohen, *The Shopping Mall High School: Winners and Losers in the Educational Marketplace* (Boston: Houghton Mifflin Company, 1985).

14. For meta-analyses of achievement effects current at the time of this writing, see Best Evidence Encyclopedia, accessed December 22, 2012, http://www .bestevidence.org. For additional perspective, see Geoffrey D. Borman, Gina M. Hewes, Laura T. Overman, and Shelly Brown, "Comprehensive School Reform and Achievement: A Meta-Analysis," *Review of Educational Research* 73 (2005): 125–230; Geoffrey D. Borman, Robert E. Slavin, Alan C. K. Cheung, Anne M. Chamberlain, Nancy A. Madden, and Betty Chambers, "Final Reading Outcomes of the National Randomized Field Trial of Success for All," *American Educational Research Journal* 44 (2007): 701–31; Comprehensive School Reform Quality Center, *CSRQ Center Report on Elementary School Comprehensive School Reform Models* (Washington, DC: American Institutes for Research, 2005); Rebecca Herman, *An Educator's Guide to Schoolwide Reform* (Arlington, VA: Educational Research Service, 1999); and James Traub, *Better by Design? A Consumer's Guide to Schoolwide Reform* (Washington, DC: Thomas Fordham Foundation, 1999).

15. See Best Evidence Encyclopedia, accessed December 22, 2012, http://www .bestevidence.org.

16. Joshua L. Glazer and Donald J. Peurach, "School Improvement Networks as a Strategy for Large Scale Reform: The Role of Educational Environments," *Educational Policy*: 1–35, accessed May 11, 2012, doi: 10.1177/08959048114 29283.

17. Eric Camburn, Brian Rowan, and James T. Taylor, "Distributed Leadership in Schools: The Case of Elementary Schools Adopting Comprehensive School Reform Models," *Educational Evaluation and Policy Analysis* 25 (2003): 347–73.

18. Brian Rowan, Richard Correnti, Robert J. Miller, and Eric M. Camburn. "School Improvement by Design: Lessons from a Study of Comprehensive School Reform Programs," in *Handbook of Education Policy Research*, ed.

Gary Sykes, Barbara Schneider, and David N. Plank (New York: Routledge, 2009).

19. See Thomas K. Glennan Jr., Susan J. Bodilly, Jolene R. Galegher, and Kerri A. Kerr, eds., *Expanding the Reach of Educational Reforms: Perspectives from Leaders in the Scale-Up of Educational Interventions* (Santa Monica, CA: Rand, 2004) and Barbara L. Schneider and Sarah-Kathryn McDonald, eds., *Scale Up in Education*, vol. 2, *Issues in Practice* (Lanham, MD: Rowman & Littlefield Publishers, 2007). For an account of the New American Schools initiative that does provide external perspective on the work of participating design teams, see Mark Berends, Susan J. Bodilly, and Sheila Nataraj Kirby, *Facing the Challenges of Whole School Reform: New American Schools after a Decade* (Santa Monica, CA: Rand, 2002).

20. For more on the use of this framework to analyze America's Choice and Success for All, see Joshua L. Glazer, "How External Interveners Leverage Large-Scale Change: The Case of America's Choice, 1998–2003," *Educational Evaluation and Policy Analysis* 31 (2009): 269–97; Donald J. Peurach, *Seeing Complexity in Public Education: Problems, Possibilities, and Success for All* (New York: Oxford University Press, 2011); and Glazer and Peurach, "School Improvement Networks."

21. See, e.g., Glennan, Bodilly, Galegher, and Kerr, *Expanding the Reach of Educational Reforms*, and Schneider and McDonald, *Scale Up in Education*.

22. Joseph P. McDonald, Emily J. Klein, and Meg Riordan, *Going to Scale with New School Designs: Reinventing High Schools* (New York: Teachers College Press, 2009).

23. Peurach, *Seeing Complexity in Public Education*.

24. For findings from the New American Schools initiative, see Berends, Bodilly, and Kirby, *Facing the Challenges of Whole School Reform*, and Glennan, Bodilly, Galegher, and Kerr, *Expanding the Reach of Educational Reforms*. For research on commercial replication, see Sidney G. Winter and Gabriel Szulanski, "Replication as Strategy," *Organization Science* 12 (2001): 730–43. For comparative research on the innovation process, see Andrew H. Van de Ven, Douglas Polley, Raghu Garud, and Sankaran Venkataraman, *The Innovation Journey* (Oxford: Oxford University Press, 1999). For a review, see Donald J. Peurach and Joshua L. Glazer, "Reconsidering Replication: New Perspectives on Large-Scale School Improvement," *Journal of Educational Change* 13 (2012): 155–90.

CHAPTER TWO

1. These are rich designs, with many possible sources of evidence, and open to many different interpretations. What we report here is not a perfect rendering of the designs as intended by the interveners. Rather, it is our interpretation of their designs, using a comprehensive but still partial subset of all available data, analyzed by ourselves and reported in our words.

2. Christine R. Finnan and Henry M. Levin, "Accelerated Schools and the Obstacles to School Reform," in *Translating Theory and Research into Educational Practice*, ed. Mark A. Constas and Robert J. Sternberg (Mahwah, NJ: Lawrence Erlbaum Associates, 2006), 137.

3. Christine R. Finnan, Edward P. St. John, Jane McCarthy, and Simeon P. Slovacek, *Accelerated Schools in Action: Lessons from the Field* (Thousand Oaks, CA: Corwin Press, Inc., 1996), 139.

4. Ibid., 22.

5. Henry M. Levin, "Learning from School Reform," (paper presented at the International Conference on Rejuvenating Schools through Partnership, Hong Kong, May 22–24, 2011), 4.

6. For an overview of the initial Accelerated Schools design, see Wendy S. Hopfenberg, Henry M. Levin, et al., *The Accelerated Schools Resource Guide* (San Francisco: Jossey-Bass Publishers, 1993). This is a trade book that describes the philosophy, transformation process, and supporting infrastructure as detailed by program developers at the start of ASP's rapid scale-up in the 1990s.

7. Finnan, St. John, McCarthy, Slovacek, *Accelerated Schools in Action*, 142.

8. Accelerated Schools Project, *Powerful Learning Framework*, pt. 2 (Palo Alto, CA: Stanford University, 1992), 3.

9. Hopfenberg, Levin, et al., *Accelerated Schools Resource Guide*.

10. Accelerated Schools Project, "Winter 1992," *Accelerated Schools* 2 (1992), 2.

11. Gene Chasin, Lisa Jaszcz, and Christine Finnan, interviewed by Karen Gates, April 5, 2007.

12. National Center for the Accelerated Schools Project, *Taking Stock Report, Expansion Section* (Palo Alto, CA: Stanford University, 1995), 9.

13. Interview with ASP executive, conducted by Karen Gates, October 28, 2004.

14. Accelerated Schools Project, "Spring 1994," *Accelerated Schools* 3 (1994), 7.

15. National Center for the Accelerated Schools Project, *Taking Stock Report, Expansion Section*, 10.

16. Kari Marble and Jennifer Stephens, "Scale-up Strategy of a National School Reform and Its Evaluation Design: Satellite Centers of the Accelerated Schools Project" (paper presented at the annual meeting of the American Educational Research Association Annual Meeting, Montreal, Canada, April 19–23, 1999).

17. Robert E. Slavin, Nancy A. Madden, Lawrence J. Dolan, and Barbara A. Wasik, *Every Child Every School: Success for All* (Thousand Oaks, CA: Corwin Press, 1996), 176–77.

18. Nancy A. Madden, Robert E. Slavin, Anna Marie Farnish, Meg Livingston, and Margarita Calderon, *Reading Wings: Teacher's Manual* (Towson, MD: Success for All Foundation, 1999), 19.

19. Meg Livingston, Nancy Cummings, and Nancy A. Madden, *Success for All Facilitator's Manual* (Baltimore, MD: Johns Hopkins University, Center for Research on the Education of Students Placed at Risk, 1996), 6–7.

20. Slavin, Madden, Dolan, and Wasik, *Every Child Every School*, 8.
21. These figures derive from Robert E. Slavin and Nancy A. Madden, *Disseminating Success for All: Lessons for Policy and Practice—Revised September 1999* (Baltimore, MD: Johns Hopkins University, Center for Research on Education for Students Placed at Risk, 1999).
22. Marc Tucker, Judy Codding, Marianne Chags, Andrea Chalmers, Phil Daro, Pat Harvey, and Sally Mentor Hayes, interviewed by David K. Cohen and Joshua L. Glazer, November 18, 1998.
23. Marc Tucker, interviewed by Joshua L. Glazer, December 1, 2005.
24. Marc Tucker, "America's Search for Successful Programs Is No Substitute for a Search for Successful Systems" (paper presented at the 2011 Meeting of the American Educational Research Association, New Orleans, LA, April 10, 2011).
25. Marc Tucker, Judy Codding, Marianne Chags, Andrea Chalmers, Phil Daro, Pat Harvey, and Sally Mentor Hayes, interviewed by David K. Cohen and Joshua L. Glazer, November 18, 1998.
26. Judith Curtis, interviewed by Joshua L. Glazer, November 30, 2005.
27. While America's Choice also has a design for math instruction, the Study of Instructional Improvement focused only on the designs for reading and writing.
28. Marc Tucker, Judy Codding, Marianne Chags, Andrea Chalmers, Phil Daro, Pat Harvey, and Sally Mentor Hayes, interviewed by David K. Cohen and Joshua L. Glazer, November 18, 1998.
29. For a detailed analysis of the knowledge needed to use the design at a high level, see Joshua L. Glazer, "Educational Professionalism: The Development of a Practice-Centered Frame and Its Application to the America's Choice School Design." PhD diss., University of Michigan, 2005.
30. The knowledge demands of the America's Choice design were elaborated by Dorothy Fowler, America's Choice director for literacy. Interviewed by Joshua L. Glazer, March 26, 2004.
31. Marc Tucker, Judy Codding, Marianne Chags, Andrea Chalmers, Phil Daro, Pat Harvey, and Sally Mentor Hayes, interviewed by David K. Cohen and Joshua L. Glazer, November 18, 1998.
32. Phil Daro, interviewed by Joshua L. Glazer, November 18, 1998.
33. Marc Tucker, Judy Codding, Marianne Chags, Andrea Chalmers, Phil Daro, Pat Harvey, and Sally Mentor Hayes, interviewed by David K. Cohen and Joshua L. Glazer, November 18, 1998.
34. In later cohorts, the America's Choice design coach was replaced by an upper-elementary literacy coordinator, while the other literacy coordinator focused on the lower grades.
35. Joshua L. Glazer, "External Efforts at District-Level Reform: The Case of the National Alliance for Restructuring Education," *Journal of Educational Change* 4 (2009): 295–314.

- 36. See Marc Tucker, "Reaching for Coherence in School Reform: The Case of America's Choice," in *Expanding the Reach of Education Reforms: What Have We Learned about Scaling Up Educational Interventions?*, ed. Thomas K. Glennan, Susan J. Bodilly, Jolene R. Gallagher, and Kerri A. Kerr (Santa Monica, CA: Rand, 2004), 197–258, and Dorothy Fowler, interviewed by Joshua L. Glazer, January 24, 2004.
- 37. AC Design Coach Training, March 9, 1999. Field notes by Joshua L. Glazer.

CHAPTER THREE

1. Howard S. Bloom, Sandra Ham, Laura Melton, Julieanne O'Brien, Fred C. Doolittle, and Susan Kagehiro, *Evaluating the Accelerated Schools Approach: A Look at Early Implementation and Impacts on Student Achievement in Eight Elementary Schools* (New York: Manpower Demonstration Research Corporation, 2001).
2. Thomas Corcoran, Margaret Hoppe, Theresa Luhm, and Jonathan A. Supovitz, *America's Choice Comprehensive School Design First-Year Implementation Evaluation Summary* (Madison, WI: Consortium for Policy Research in Education, 2000).
3. Robert E. Slavin and Nancy A. Madden, *One Million Children: Success for All* (Thousand Oaks, CA: Corwin Press, 2001), 272, 301.
4. Geoffrey Borman, Gina M. Hewes, Laura T. Overman, and Shelly Brown, "Comprehensive School Reform and Achievement: A Meta-Analysis," *Review of Educational Research* 73 (2003): 125–230.
5. Barbara Haxby (SFA director of implementation), pers. comm. with Donald J. Peurach, June 24, 2005.
6. Amanda Datnow, "Power and Politics in the Adoption of Whole-School Reform Models," *Educational Evaluation and Policy Analysis* 22 (2000): 357–74.
7. Nancy A. Madden, interviewed by Donald J. Peurach, April 10, 2003.
8. SFA trainer, interviewed by Donald J. Peurach, March 27, 2009.
9. For more on interpretations of formal programs and structures in Success for All as bureaucratic, technocratic, and/or professional, see Donald J. Peurach, *Seeing Complexity in Public Education: Problems, Possibilities, and Success for All* (New York: Oxford University Press, 2011), chaps. 1 and 2.
10. Robert Slavin, interviewed by Donald J. Peurach, March 27, 2003.
11. SFA manager, interviewed by Donald J. Peurach, April 13, 2003.
12. Barbara Haxby, interviewed by Donald J. Peurach, April 14, 2003.
13. Ibid.
14. Jonathan A. Supovitz, Susan M. Poglinco, and Amy Bach, *Implementation of the America's Choice Literacy Workshops* (Philadelphia: Consortium for Policy Research in Education, 2002), 6.
15. Marc Tucker, "Reaching for Coherence in School Reform: The Case of America's Choice," in *Expanding the Reach of Education Reforms: What Have We Learned about Scaling Up Educational Interventions?*, ed. Thomas K. Glen-

nan, Susan J. Bodilly, Jolene R. Gallagher, and Kerri A. Kerr (Santa Monica, CA: Rand, 2004), 245.

16. America's Choice Literacy Institute no. 4, June 14, 1999. Field notes by Joshua L. Glazer.

17. Mary Ann Mays, Sally Mentor Hay, Tony Trujillo, Judy Aaronson, Phil Daro, Marge Sable, Judy Codding, Sally Hampton, and Marc Tucker, interviewed by David K. Cohen and Joshua L. Glazer, September 24, 1999.

18. Dorothy Fowler, interviewed by Joshua L. Glazer, January 24, 2002.

19. Ibid.

20. Marc Tucker, interviewed by Joshua L. Glazer, December 1, 2005.

21. Larry Molinaro, interviewed by Joshua L. Glazer, November 26, 2005.

22. Peter Hill, interviewed by Joshua L. Glazer, September 26, 2002.

23. Larry Molinaro, interviewed by Joshua L. Glazer, November 26, 2005.

24. Ibid.

25. America's Choice cluster leader, interviewed by Joshua L. Glazer, October 23, 2000.

26. Tucker, "Reaching for Coherence in School Reform," 234.

27. Susan Fitzgerald, interviewed by Joshua L. Glazer, January 24, 2002.

28. Pilar Soler and Henry M. Levin, "Obstacles to Inquiry" (paper presented at National Networking Meeting of Accelerated Schools Project, St. Louis, January 31–February 1, 1997).

29. Christine Finnan, Katherine C. Schnepel, and Lorin W. Anderson, "Powerful Learning Environments," *Journal of Education for Students Placed at Risk* (2003): 391–418.

30. Kari Marble and Jennifer Stephens, "Scale-up Strategy of a National School Reform and Its Evaluation Design: Satellite Centers of the Accelerated Schools Project," (paper presented at the annual meeting of the American Educational Research Association Annual Meeting, Montreal, Canada, April 19–23, 1999), 5.

31. Ibid., 16.

32. Ibid., 2.

33. As reported in chaps. 4 and 5, in the mid-2000s, decisions by ASP's National Center to place tighter controls on the commitment of participating schools interacted with other conditions to drive a dramatic reduction in the ASP network, from 1,400 schools to approximately 250 schools.

34. For example, see Bloom, Ham, Melton, O'Brien, Doolittle, and Kagehiro, *Evaluating the Accelerated Schools Approach*. Bloom et al. report that "staff in nearly all the sample schools cited lack of sufficient time as a key challenge to sustaining implementation of the Accelerated Schools approach to governance and decision-making" (p. 29).

35. Christine R. Finnan and Henry M. Levin, "Accelerated Schools and the Obstacles to School Reform," in *Translating Theory and Research into Educational Practice*, ed. Mark A. Constas and Robert J. Sternberg (Mahwah, NJ: Lawrence Erlbaum Associates, 2006), 140.

36. Bloom, Ham, Melton, O'Brien, Doolittle, and Kagehiro, *Evaluating the Accelerated Schools Approach*, 37.

37. Henry M. Levin, "Learning from School Reform" (paper presented at the International Conference on Rejuvenating Schools through Partnership, Hong Kong, May 22–24, 2001). As reported in the paper, "some leaders have enthusiasm, commitment, and skills to support a move to inquiry and powerful learning. Others are less open to change and embrace the existing school culture so completely that they will not make much effort to engage and lead the process. Good leadership must be continuous in supporting day-to-day application of the ASP process, inquiry, and powerful learning. It must be active and passionate. . . . Most of the skills can be taught, but not the commitment, passion, and interpersonal support . . . differences in leadership are important causes of difference in school success [in implementing ASP]" (22).

38. The first gathering of this type, a "Principals' Academy," was offered during the summer of 2002 by the National Center for the Accelerated Schools Project at the University of Connecticut, Storrs, CT.

39. Marble and Stephens, "Scale-up Strategy of a National School Reform," 20.

40. Missouri Accelerated Schools Project, March 21–22, 2001. Field notes by Karen Gates. One other element of nonadherence was that the satellite was not using .25 external coaches from district offices, for which the national model called but did not require. The satellite's decision to dedicate full-time staff with experience in ASP schools might have been operationally better and more feasible.

41. Gene Chasin (director, National Center for AS Plus), interviewed by Karen Gates, April 8, 2004. Henry M. Levin remained affiliated as founder, though informally and not as a member of the new external advisory board discussed in the following chapter.

42. Finnan and Levin, "Accelerated Schools and the Obstacles to School Reform," 135.

43. Marble and Stephens, "Scale-up Strategy of a National School Reform."

44. Ibid., 5.

45. National Center for the Accelerated Schools Project, *Taking Stock Report, Expansion Section*, 10.

46. Marble and Stephens, "Scale-up Strategy of a National School Reform and its Evaluation Design: Satellite Centers of the Accelerated Schools Project," 19, 22.

47. Arthur Levine, *Educating School Teachers* (Washington, DC: Education Schools Project, 2006).

CHAPTER FOUR

1. The pattern of activity reported here is consistent with broader theory and research on the innovation process and on franchise-like commercial

replication. See Donald J. Peurach, *Seeing Complexity in Public Education: Problems, Possibilities, and Success for All* (New York: Oxford University Press, 2011) and Donald J. Peurach and Joshua L. Glazer, "Reconsidering Replication: New Perspectives on Large-Scale School Improvement," *Journal of Educational Change* 13 (2012): 155–90.

2. Gene Chasin (director, National Center for AS Plus), interviewed by Karen Gates, July 18, 2003.

3. Gene Chasin (director, National Center for AS Plus), interviewed by Karen Gates, April 8, 2004.

4. National Center for AS Plus, *TRACES—Tools for Reflection, Assessment, and Continuous Evaluation of Schools*, Version 2.0 (Storrs, CT: National Center for AS Plus, 2005): 5.

5. Gene Chasin (director, National Center for AS Plus), interviewed by Karen Gates, November 4, 2005.

6. ASP executive, interviewed by Karen Gates, April 8, 2004.

7. Gene Chasin, *Lessons Learned: Providing Local Support to Schools Sites, Accelerated Schools Plus* (Storrs, CT: National Center for AS Plus, 2005); National Center for the Accelerated Schools Project, *ASP Design Overview* (Storrs, CT: National Center for AS Plus, 2003), 7.

8. National Center for AS Plus, *TRACES*, 8–10.

9. Chasin, *Lessons Learned*, 16.

10. National Center for the Accelerated Schools Project, *ASP Design Overview*, 7.

11. AS Plus Network Meeting Retreat, October 28–29, 2004. Field notes by Karen Gates.

12. Gene Chasin (director, National Center for AS Plus), interviewed by Karen Gates, April 8, 2004.

13. AS Plus Regional Conference, November 13–14, 2003. Field notes by Karen Gates.

14. Gene Chasin (director, National Center for AS Plus), interviewed by Karen Gates, April 8, 2004.

15. Ibid.

16. Ibid.

17. ASP executives, interviewed by Karen Gates, April 5, 2007.

18. Chasin, *Lessons Learned*, 17.

19. AS Plus Regional Conference, November 13–14, 2003. Field notes by Karen Gates.

20. ASP executive, interviewed by Karen Gates, April 8, 2004.

21. Gene Chasin (director, National Center for AS Plus), interviewed by Karen Gates, April 8, 2004.

22. AS Plus Network Meeting Retreat, October 28–29, 2004. Field notes by Karen Gates.

23. AS Plus Regional Network Meeting, June 14, 2006. Field notes by Karen Gates.

24. Christine R. Finnan and Henry M. Levin, "Accelerated Schools and the Obstacles to School Reform," in *Translating Theory and Research into Educational Practice*, ed. Mark A. Constas and Robert J. Sternberg (Mahwah, NJ: Lawrence Erlbaum Associates, 2006), 143.

25. Gene Chasin (director, National Center for AS Plus), interviewed by Karen Gates, April 8, 2004.

26. For additional details about these three frameworks, see Peurach, *Seeing Complexity in Public Education*.

27. Success for All's "Change Process" framework drew directly from Bruce W. Tuckman, "Developmental Sequence in Small Groups," *Psychological Bulletin* 63 (1965): 384–99. Also, SFA's "Stages of Concern" and "Levels of Use" frameworks derived directly from the Concerns Based Adoption Model. See Shirley M. Hord, William L. Rutherford, Leslie Huling-Austin, and Gene E. Hall, *Taking Charge of Change* (Alexandria, VA: Association for Curriculum and Development, 1987).

28. Success for All Foundation, *Success for All—Reading First: Fulfilling the Requirements of the Reading First Legislation* (Towson, MD: Success for All Foundation, 2002), 1.

29. Barbara Haxby (SFAF director of implementation), interviewed by Donald J. Peurach, April 14, 2003.

30. Ibid.

31. Twenty of the schools were elementary schools, and twenty were middle schools.

32. Janice McClure, interviewed by Joshua L. Glazer, October 27, 2004.

33. Marc Tucker, interviewed by Joshua L. Glazer, September 19, 2006. Tucker reported that, with respect to Georgia, "the whole effort has been a capacity-building effort in that we have, from the start, trained central and regional staff to provide the training, professional development, and technical assistance needed to implement our program on a very large scale."

34. Ibid.

35. Marc Tucker, "Reaching for Coherence in School Reform: The Case of America's Choice," in *Expanding the Reach of Education Reforms: What Have We Learned about Scaling Up Educational Interventions?*, ed. Thomas K. Glennan, Susan J. Bodilly, Jolene R. Gallagher, and Kerri A. Kerr (Santa Monica, CA: Rand, 2004), 235.

36. Janice McClure, interviewed by Joshua L. Glazer, October 27, 2004.

37. Marc Tucker, interviewed by Joshua L. Glazer, January 12, 2005; Judy Aronson, interviewed by Joshua L. Glazer, November 28, 2005; Henry May, Jonathan A. Supovitz, and Joy Lesnick, *The Impact of America's Choice on Writing Performance in Georgia: First-Year Results* (Madison, WI: Consortium for Policy Research in Education, 2004).

38. Carol A. Barnes, Dianne Massell, and Charles Vanover, *Building District Capacity: The Interplay of Environments, District Management and Designs in*

Taking Instructional Improvement to Scale In High Poverty Schools (Ann Arbor: University of Michigan, 2007), 26.

39. Regarding Jacksonville, see Jonathan Supovitz, Brook S. Taylor, and Henry May, *The Impact of America's Choice on Student Performance in X County, Florida* (Madison, WI: Consortium for Policy Research in Education, 2002). The authors note the possibility that "the implementation of elements of the America's Choice design in other schools in Duval County through the district's standards-based reform efforts are reducing the differences between the performance of America's Choice schools and other district schools because other district schools are also improving in performance" (16). Regarding Georgia, see May, Supovitz, and Lesnick, *The Impact of America's Choice on Writing Performance in Georgia*, 9.

40. Janice McClure, interviewed by Joshua L. Glazer, October 27, 2004.

41. Barnes, Massell, and Vanover, *Building District Capacity*. The authors argued that it was "exceptionally challenging" for district staff to monitor and support implementation, and that district leaders lacked the capability to deeply understand the design and remake leadership to support implementation (26).

42. AC staff member, interviewed by Joshua L. Glazer, November 27, 2005.

43. Larry Molinaro, interviewed by Joshua L. Glazer, August 9, 2006.

44. Janice McClure, e-mail message to Joshua L. Glazer, August 3, 2006.

45. Judy Aronson, interviewed by Joshua L. Glazer, May 14, 2007.

46. Judy Aronson, interviewed by Joshua L. Glazer, November 28, 2005.

47. Larry Molinaro, interviewed by Joshua L. Glazer, August 9, 2006.

48. Tucker, "Reaching for Coherence in School Reform," 235.

49. Larry Molinaro, interviewed by Joshua L. Glazer, November 26, 2005.

50. Brian Rowan, Richard Correnti, Robert J. Miller, and Eric M. Camburn. "School Improvement by Design: Lessons from a Study of Comprehensive School Reform Programs," in *Handbook of Education Policy Research*, ed. Gary Sykes, Barbara Schneider, and David N. Plank (New York: Routledge, 2009).

CHAPTER FIVE

1. Larry Molinaro, interviewed by Joshua L. Glazer, May 15, 2007.

2. Judy Aaronson, interviewed by Joshua L. Glazer, May 14, 2007.

3. Judy Coding, interviewed by Joshua L. Glazer, May 17, 2007.

4. Marc Tucker, interviewed by Joshua L. Glazer, December 1, 2005.

5. National Center on Education and the Economy, *Tough Times or Tough Choices: The Report of the New Commission on the Skills of the American Workforce* (San Francisco: Jossey-Bass, 2007).

6. Ibid., 70.

7. Marc Tucker, interviewed by Joshua L. Glazer, December 1, 2005.

8. Judy Codding, interviewed by Joshua L. Glazer, May 5, 2007.
9. Judy Aaronson, interviewed by Joshua L. Glazer, May 14, 2007.
10. Ibid.
11. Larry Molinaro, interviewed by Joshua L. Glazer, May 15, 2007.
12. Success for All cofounder Robert Slavin described this new market as the "district coherence" market. See Robert E. Slavin, "Change Schools, Change Districts? How the Two Approaches Can Work Together," *Education Week* 22, no. 25 (2003): 44–64.
13. Robert Slavin, interviewed by Donald J. Peurach, March 27, 2003.
14. See Geoffrey Borman, Gina M. Hewes, Laura T. Overman, and Shelly Brown, "Comprehensive School Reform and Achievement: A Meta-Analysis," *Review of Educational Research* 73 (2003): 125–230, and also Geoffrey D. Borman, Robert E. Slavin, Alan Cheung, Anne Chamberlain, Nancy A. Madden, and Bette Chambers, "Final Reading Outcomes of the National Randomized Field Trial of Success for All," *American Educational Research Journal* 44 (2007): 701–31.
15. US Department of Education, Office of the Inspector General, *The Reading First Program's Grant Application Process: Final Inspection Report.* (Washington, DC: US Department of Education, 2006), 2.
16. US Government Accountability Office, *Reading First: States Report Improvements in Reading Instruction, but Additional Procedures Would Clarify Education's Role in Ensuring Proper Implementation by States* (Washington, DC: United States Government Accountability Office, 2007).
17. Debra Viadaro, " 'Scientific' Label in Law Stirs Debate: Proposals Could Reduce Focus on Randomized Experiments," *Education Week* 27, no. 8 (2007): 1–23.
18. SFA staff member, interviewed by Donald J. Peurach, March 8, 2004.
19. ASP executives, interviewed by Karen Gates, April 5, 2007.
20. Gene Chasin (Director, National Center, Accelerated Schools Plus), interviewed by Karen Gates, April 5, 2007.
21. ASP executive, interviewed by Karen Gates, April 8, 2004.
22. Gene Chasin (director, National Center for AS Plus), interviewed by Karen Gates, April 29, 2006.
23. Gene Chasin (director, National Center for AS Plus), interviewed by Karen Gates, July 31, 2008.
24. University of Connecticut Neag School of Education, accessed December 22, 2009, http://www.education.uconn.edu/research/commpact/index .cfm.
25. AS Plus executive, interviewed by Karen Gates, July 31, 2008.
26. Ibid.
27. The number of 240 schools was reported by Gene Chasin (director, National Center, AS Plus) at a seminar titled, "Lessons Learned about School Improvement from Comprehensive School Reform Providers," offered by the University of Michigan's Interdisciplinary Committee on Organiza-

tional Studies, November 10, 2006. The number of 180 schools was reported by Chasin in an interview conducted by Karen Gates, July 31, 2008.

28. Gene Chasin (director, National Center for AS Plus), interviewed by Karen Gates, July 31, 2008.

29. Brian Rowan, Richard Correnti, Robert J. Miller, and Eric M. Camburn. "School Improvement by Design: Lessons from a Study of Comprehensive School Reform Programs," in *Handbook of Education Policy Research*, ed. Gary Sykes, Barbara Schneider, and David N. Plank (New York: Routledge, 2009). AS Plus, the revised and much reduced version of ASP, ended its mid-2000s improvement cycle—several years after our colleagues' data was collected—reporting that 90% of its schools were making adequate yearly progress.

CHAPTER SIX

1. Peter Hill, interviewed by Joshua Glazer, January 24, 2002.

2. Andrew Van de Ven, Douglas E. Polley, Raghu Garud, and Sankaran Venkataraman, *The Innovation Journey* (Oxford: Oxford University Press, 1999). In their large study of private and public sector innovation, Van de Ven et al. report that this supportive infrastructure is the essential determinant of successful innovation.

3. Marshall S. Smith and Jennifer O'Day, "Systemic School Reform," in *The Politics of Curriculum and Testing: The 1990 Yearbook of the Politics of Education Association*, ed. Susan H. Fuhrman and Betty Malen (New York: Falmer Press, 1991).

4. The three organizations did not speak or write about educational infrastructure, but about teaching, organization, curriculum, and the like. Nonetheless, we believe that our language fairly represents their initiatives.

5. This problem is discussed in more detail in David K. Cohen and Susan L. Moffitt, *The Ordeal of Equality* (Cambridge, MA: Harvard University Press, 2009), chap. 2.

6. This information was accessed December 22, 2012, at http://www.bestevidence.org.

7. Gene Chasin and Christine Finnan, interviewed by David K. Cohen and Karen Gates, July 27, 2006. Chasin and Finnan told us that the weak results that SII found were the result of the recruitment of many schools that were weakly engaged with the intervention. They report that with fewer, more engaged schools, AS Plus has a greater effect on teaching and learning.

8. Frederick M. Hess, "Back to School," *The American: The Journal of the American Enterprise Institute*, accessed April 24, 2008, http://www.american.com/archive/2008/april-04-08/back-to-school.

9. Richard J. Murnane and Richard R. Nelson, "Improving the Performance of the Education Sector: The Valuable, Challenging, and Limited Role of

Random Assignment Evaluations," *Economics of Innovation and New Technology* 16 (2007): 307–22.

10. Anthony S. Bryk, "Support a Science of Performance Improvement," *Phi Delta Kappan* 90 (2009): 597–600.

APPENDIX

1. See Donald J. Peurach, *Designing and Managing Comprehensive School Reform: The Case of Success for All*. PhD diss., University of Michigan, 2005; Donald J. Peurach, *Seeing Complexity in Public Education: Problems, Possibilities, and Success for All* (New York: Oxford University Press, 2011); Donald J. Peurach and Joshua L. Glazer, "Reconsidering Replication: New Perspectives on Large-Scale School Improvement," *Journal of Educational Change* 13 (2012): 155–90; and Joshua L. Glazer and Donald J. Peurach, "School Improvement Networks as a Strategy for Large Scale Reform: The Role of Educational Environments," *Educational Policy*: 1–35, accessed May 11, 2012, doi: 10.1177/0895904811429283.

2. See Joshua L. Glazer, "Educational Professionalism: The Development of a Practice-Centered Frame and Its Application to the America's Choice School Design." PhD diss., University of Michigan, 2005; Joshua L. Glazer, Educational Professionalism: An Inside-Out View, *American Journal of Education* 114 (2008): 169–89; Joshua L. Glazer, "External Efforts at District-Level Reform: The Case of the National Alliance for Restructuring Education," *Journal of Educational Change* 4 (2009): 295–314; and Joshua L. Glazer, "How External Interveners Leverage Large-Scale Change: The Case of America's Choice, 1998–2003," *Educational Evaluation and Policy Analysis* 31 (2009): 269–97.

3. David K. Cohen and Susan L. Moffitt, *The Ordeal of Equality: Can Federal Regulation Fix the Schools?* (Cambridge, MA: Harvard University Press, 2009).

Index

Aaronson, Judy, 140–41
Abbott, Andrew, 194
AC. *See* America's Choice (AC)
Accelerated Schools Project (ASP):
assessment process and, 97,
98–99, 100; branding and,
102–3; comprehensiveness of,
18–19; consortium of process-
based schools and, 101; controls
on participating schools and,
205n33; core ambition of, 61;
core strategy of, 29–30, 80, 83,
85–86; culture versus instruction and, 38; data collection
and, 85; decentralization and,
33, 35, 37–38, 85–87, 91; demonstration sites and, 97–98;
design improvements in, 98–99;
from design to practice in,
56–57, 58; district buy-in and,
97; early development of, 1;
effectiveness of, 19, 177–78;
environmental resources and,
45–46; evaluation of, 60, 165; as
example of success, xi–xii; external and internal coaches and,
32–33; fees owed to, 87; formal
contracting with partners and,
97; founding of, 8; incoherence
within, 86–87; instructional
guidance in, 50; Leadership
Academy of, 99; leadership
changes at, 85, 206n41; literature on design of, 202n6; local
organizational networks and,
30; low-level versus high-level

enactment and, 81, 83, 86, 88,
96; national faculty of, 99–100;
new vision for, 96; number
of schools in, 31; open design
of, 7, 8–9, 28, 31–34; organizational features of, 12–13;
organizational restructuring of,
99–102; organizational structure
of schools in, 32–33; participant-
observation at, 189–90; participative decision making in, 31;
as path of least resistance, 83;
performance goals of, 2; position of, in US education, 59;
powerful learning and, 32, 33;
provider centers and, 99–100,
101; quality of leaders and,
206n37; rapid growth of, 82–83;
reduction in network of, 205n33;
satellite organizations and, 36–
38, 81–87, 96–97, 99, 101–3,
206n40; scale of, 2; School as a
Whole (SAW) and, 32; school
environments and, 35–38;
schools' enlistment in, 30–31,
81, 82–83, 97; SII study and, 185,
187, 191, 192–93, 197–98; site-
based management and, 28;
staff size and, 100; strengths-
based approach of, 29, 39, 81;
sustainability of, 30; time required for, 83–84, 205n34;
training for leaders and, 99;
training for principals in, 84,
206n38; training materials and,
33–34; validity

and, 158–60, 162; Instructional Audit
and, 156, 158; instructional infrastructure and, 165; Leadership Academy of,
156; longevity in program and, 161;
loss of satellites and, 103; NCLB and,
104–6, 154–56, 157–58, 160–61; number of schools in, 155–56, 160–61, 162,
210–11n27; participant-observation at,
190; progress of schools in, 173; rapid
expansion of, 174; reduced network size
and, 174; schools' adoption of, 104–5;
school selection and, 155–56, 157; staffing levels and, 173; strengths-based
approach of, 156; time required for, 154,
158; training programs' demands on,
161–62; widespread use of, xii. *See also*
Accelerated Schools Project (ASP)
assessment: as detached from curriculum,
171; interveners' success and, 60; lack
of, in comprehensive school reform, 19;
as weak guide to practice, 176
Atlas Communities of Schools, 159–60

Ball, Deborah Loewenberg, xiii
Barnes, Carol A., 209n41
basic skills, versus critical thinking, 2
Benchmarking for Success, Common Core
and, ix–x, 20
Best Evidence Encyclopedia, 149, 152
Bloom, Howard S., 205n34
Bush, George W., and Bush administration,
19, 137, 171, 182–83

Calkins, Lucy, 50
Carriedo, Ruben, 186
CCSSI (Common Core State Standards Ini-
tiative). *See* Common Core Initiative
CDDRE. *See* Center for Data Driven Reform
in Education (CDDRE)
Center for Data Driven Reform in Education
(CDDRE), 147, 149–50
Center for Gifted and Talented Education
(University of Connecticut), 101
Center for Research and Reform in Educa-
tion (CRRE), 147
Center for the Social Organization of
Schools (Johns Hopkins University), 7
Center for the Study of Students Placed at
Risk, 7
charter schools: AS Plus and, 156, 160–61;
comprehensive school reform and,

180–81; as focus of federal policy, 183;
ideal scale of networks and, 181; management organizations and, 179; versus
transformation of existing schools,
11–12
Chasin, Gene: on AS Plus versus NCLB,
154; on ASP's school-based support
model, 102; on assessment of AS Plus,
211n7; on capacity building, 157; on
consortium of process-based schools,
101; on cultural transformation, 34; as
director of ASP, 85; IUSI and, 159; lobbying by, 160; new vision for ASP and, 96;
on number of schools in AS Plus, 210–
11n27; on policy pendulum, 162–63; on
size of AS Plus, 156; on strengths-based
approach, 156; on strengths in ASP
organization, 100
Clinton, Bill, and Clinton administration,
171, 182–83
Codding, Judy: AC's early days and, 126;
AC's for-profit status and, 140; AC's
Navigator program, 136; on limits of
AC's unbundled solutions, 139; on
teachers in AC, 51
Cohen, David K., 186, 194
Common Core Initiative: anticipated problems with, 170, 176; gathering movement for, 163; idea underlying, ix–x;
intersection of forces in work of, 20;
launch of, 153; learning from interveners and, 179–80; limitations of, 178;
reasons for hope and caution about, x;
schools' and systems' likely response and,
x–xi; types of organizations suitable for,
180–81; uncertainties surrounding, 167;
as unprecedented, ix
CommPACT Schools, 159–60
comprehensive school reform: Common
Core Initiative and, 180–81; confidence
in, 107; district- and state-level operations and, 181, 182–83; funding streams
for schools and, 83, 117, 152, 153; ideal
scale of networks and, 181; improved
likelihood of success and, 178–79; intervening organizations necessary for,
183; meaning of *comprehensive* and, 174;
NCLB and, 4, 107, 110–11; networks of
supporting, 181; New American Schools
initiative and, 165; pressure on SFA and,
65; qualified success of, 18–19; as SFA

comprehensive school reform (*cont.*)
program, 111; SFA's work in Washington and, 110; versus targeted interventions, 132–36, 138–40, 145–46, 150–51, 155–57, 161–62, 167; time required for, 174, 177; turbulence in niche market for, 131–33; turnaround schools and, 179; waning market for, 162. *See also* school reform
Comprehensive School Reform Demonstration Act (1997), 65
Concerns Based Adoption Model, 208n27
Consortium for Policy Research in Education (CPRE), 185
Core Knowledge (school reform project), 19, 178, 187
Council of Chief State School Officers, 20, 153
CPRE. *See* Consortium for Policy Research in Education (CPRE)
craft coherence, unequal distribution of, xi
critical thinking, versus basic skills, 2
CRRE. *See* Center for Research and Reform in Education (CRRE)
CSRD. *See* Obey-Porter Comprehensive School Reform Demonstration Act (CSRD, 1997)
curriculum: assessments as detached from, 171; innovations of 1950s and 1960s and, 15–16, 17–18
Curtis, Judith, 136

Daro, Phil, 49, 50, 51
design puzzle: AC and, 28, 49–53, 57–58, 116–17, 119–20; ambitions of interveners and, 27; ASP and, 28, 31–34, 56–57, 58, 96–101; AS Plus and, 155–60; comprehensive school reform versus targeted interventions and, 134–36, 145–46; as core puzzle of improvement by design, 22; design versus practice and, 56–59, 186; growing complexity and, 174; integrity of design and, 123–24; interpretations of, 201n1; interveners' originality and, 172–73; market for school improvement and, 133–34; SFA and, 28, 40–43, 57–58, 106–9, 112; weak schools and, 27–28, 107. *See also* improvement by design
Direct Instruction (school reform project), 19, 178

dot-com boom and bust, 4, 45, 93, 114, 131, 166

economic collapse of 2008, 153
Educational Research and Development to Improve Achievement Act (2007), 148
Elementary and Secondary Education Act (ESEA), 4, 46, 114. *See also* Title I of Elementary and Secondary Education Act (ESEA)
evaluation. *See* assessment
expectations of students, 12

federal grants to states, 3
Finnan, Christine, 83–84, 211n7
First Things First, 19, 178
Fowler, Dorothy, 74–75, 76

Gates, Karen, 186, 188, 189–90, 192–93, 198
Georgia, AC's work in, 118, 121, 124–25, 208n33
gifted and talented students, 29, 32
Glazer, Joshua, 186, 188, 189, 191–92, 193–94
Goals 2000: Educate America Act (1994), x, 3, 65
Goldin, Simona, 186
Graves, Donald, 50

Harcourt, 144
Hatch, Thomas, xi
Hawkins-Stafford Amendments (1988), 3
Haxby, Barbara, 70, 71–72, 112, 114
Hewlett Foundation, 182
Hill, Peter, 77, 171
Honig, Meredith, xi

i3 program. *See* Investing in Innovation (i3)
IDEA, 179
IEE. *See* Institute for Effective Education (IEE)
implementation puzzle: AC's training organization and, 125–26; competing initiatives and, 73–74; continuity amid change and, 99; coordination required for, 62; as core puzzle of improvement by design, 23; demands on teachers and, 74–75; design versus practice and, 56–59; district and state involvement and, 121–25, 126–27, 128, 166, 209n41;

school-based, 119. *See also* professional development

teacher quality: clustering of weak teachers and, 73; education of teachers and, 5, 12; in high-poverty schools, 3, 12; lax certification standards and, 66; subject-area knowledge and, 16; teachers' need for guidance and, 76; uncertified teachers and, 66

Title I of Elementary and Secondary Education Act (ESEA): budget appropriations and, 141; demand for school improvement and, 166–67; funding and, 3–4; interveners' reliance on, 59, 175; policy and practice and, 194; pressure on Success for All and, 65; private and public forces in school reform and, 167; school improvement for disadvantaged children and, 18; schools' reliance on, 152; school-wide reading curricula and, 28; SFA and, 39, 40, 46, 107; support for interveners via, 13

Tucker, Marc: on AC's adaptations, 138–39; on AC's decentralization, 121; AC's early days and, 126; on AC's Georgia work, 209n39; on AC's reorganization as for-profit, 137; on AC's training services, 125; founding of AC and, 9; funding

for AC and, 55; on large-scale education reform, 73; on local adaptation of AC's design, 123; reform advocacy of, 137–38; on school improvement market, 133; on systemic challenges, 118–19; on teachers' need for guidance, 76; on travel costs for AC, 79; on working at scale, 48

Tuckman, Bruce W., 208n27

turnaround schools, 156, 179

University of Connecticut: ASP and, 8, 99, 100; Atlas Communities of Schools and, 159–60; Center for Gifted and Talented Education at, 101; CommPact Schools and, 159–60; IUSI and, 158–60

University of Pittsburgh, 9, 50, 53

University of York (UK), 147

US Department of Education, 147–48

Van de Ven, Andrew H., 211n2

Vanover, Charles, 209n41

Weiss, Christopher, 186

What Works Clearinghouse, 149, 152

whole-school reform, 4, 9

William T. Grant Foundation, 182

working conditions, 58